THE ECONOMIC CONSEQUENCES OF QUEBEC SOVEREIGNTY

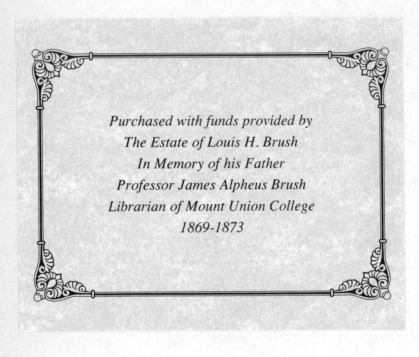

THE ECONOMIC CONSEQUENCES OF QUEBEC SOVEREIGNTY

by
PATRICK GRADY

The Fraser Institute
Vancouver, British Columbia, Canada

Canadian Cataloguing in Publication Data

Grady, Patrick Michael.
The economic consequences of Quebec sovereignty

Includes bibliographical references.
ISBN 0-88975-137-4

1. Quebec (Province)—Economic conditions—
1960–ㅤ*ㅤ2. Quebec (Province)—Economic
policy. 3. Quebec (Province)—History—
Autonomy and independence movements. 4.
Federal-provincial fiscal relations—Quebec
(Province).* 5. Federal-provincial fiscal
relations—Canada.* I. Fraser Institute
(Vancouver, B.C.). II. Title.
HC117.Q4G73 1991ㅤ330.9714'04ㅤC91-091693-4

330.9714
G 733e

Printed in Canada.

The events of the coming year will not be shaped by the deliberate act of statesmen, but by the hidden currents, flowing continually beneath the surface of political history, of which no one can predict the outcome. In only one way can we influence these hidden currents,—by setting in motion those forces of instruction and imagination which change *opinion*. The assertion of truth, the unveiling of illusion, the dissipation of hate, the enlargement and instruction of men's hearts and minds, must be the means.

John Maynard Keynes
The Economic Consequences of the Peace
(1920, pp. 296-7)

Acknowledgements

TO MY WIFE JEAN AND my grandfather Irish.

Table of Contents

Tables and Figures

List of Tables

List of Figures

Preface

PRIME MINISTER MULRONEY ASKED in his February 13th Quebec speech (Office of the Prime Minister, 1991b) if any business person would be prepared to put the future of their company on the line without an in-depth cost/benefit analysis or market study and if the future of the country did not deserve at the very least equally serious analysis. He stressed that "it is not economic blackmail to ask Quebeckers to look carefully at the facts before taking economic decisions that involve their economic well-being and that of their children." The Citizens' Forum characterized Canadians as "shockingly ill-informed" about the economic costs of Quebec independence (1991b, p.119).

In spite of the current information vacuum on the economic consequences of Quebec sovereignty, a consensus based on wishful thinking has emerged among many Québécois economists and businesspeople and has been enshrined as dogma in the reports of the Allaire Committee and the Bélanger-Campeau Commission. In the long run, they argue, there are no economic costs to sovereignty and the short-run transitional costs can be minimized if both sides to the split behave rationally. This consensus is challenged by the facts presented in this study.

Quebeckers need to take a much harder look at the economic benefits from Confederation and the costs of separation. If they did, they would learn how much they stand to lose. Perhaps then they would become less willing to gamble their economic future on sovereigntist wishful thinking. Similarly, if English Canadians were to examine seriously the costs of Quebec separation they would see that Quebeckers would not be the only losers.

This study deals only with the economics of Quebec sovereignty and does not consider the larger question of the constitutional options for renewed federalism. But this does not mean that I do not have strong views on the need for constitutional renewal. Indeed, I urge my fellow Canadians to go the extra mile necessary to accommodate Quebec's legitimate demands in the upcoming constitutional round. The country cannot afford another Meech Lake debacle. Canada is too great a country to be broken up by narrow-minded stubbornness. With good will and rationality on both sides, there is no reason why we cannot reach an agreement that will be beneficial to all Canadians and will build a better country.

About the Author

PATRICK GRADY IS A PARTNER in Global Economics Ltd., an Ottawa economic consulting firm and an Adjunct Scholar of the Fraser Institute. He received a Ph.D. in economics from the University of Toronto in 1973 and a B.A. from the University of Illinois in 1968.

Though he is not from Quebec, he has had a special interest in and affection for Quebec since his youth. He was raised on his grandfather Irish's tales of growing up on the family farm in St.-Basile outside of Quebec City and of working in Quebec lumber camps. As a student, he spent two summers in Quebec City, one of which was spent studying French at Laval University in the old Séminaire du Québec. Dr. Grady was also an economic consultant to a Montreal investment dealer in 1982 and 1983.

Dr. Grady has written widely on economic policy, macroeconomics, and public finance. His writings have appeared in the *Canadian Journal of Economics*, the *Canadian Tax Journal*, *Canadian Public Policy*, the *Canadian Journal of Program Evaluation*, *L'Actualité Economique*, *Canadian Forum*, *Policy Options*, the *Journal of Empirical Economics*, *Globe and Mail*, the *Financial Post*, and the *Montreal Gazette*. He also edited *Peering Under the Inflationary Veil* for the Economic Council of Canada. His study on "The State of the Art of Canadian Macroeconomic Modelling" was released by the Department of Finance and has become a standard reference source on model structure.

From 1972 to 1981 Dr. Grady held various positions in Ottawa, including Research Officer in charge of economic forecasting at the Bank of Canada and Director of Fiscal Policy in the Department of Finance.

In 1981 he resigned from the public service to establish his own economic consulting firm, Grady Economics Ltd. From 1981 to 1986 he practised as a consultant. On one consulting assignment, Dr. Grady served as Project Director for the Economic Council of Canada's Annual Review for 1982, *Lean Times*. He also worked for the Macdonald Commission on the economy as a member of the team which drafted part of its final report dealing with economic growth and employment.

In July 1986 Dr. Grady accepted a two-year term appointment to serve as the first Director of the new Economic Analysis and Forecasting Division in the Department of Finance. At the end of his term in June 1988, he returned to consulting and co-founded Global Economics Ltd.

Chapter 1

Canada at the
Cross Roads

National crisis

CANADA IS NOW IN THE THROES of its most serious national crisis. Federalists and sovereigntists are struggling over the constitutional future of Quebec. Faced with the prospect of a Canada without Quebec and a Quebec without Canada, Canadians across the country are being forced to consider the economic consequences of Quebec sovereignty for both Quebec and Canada.

The build-up to the present crisis came surprisingly quickly. Quebec had never agreed to the new Canadian Constitution which was patriated from the United Kingdom in 1982. The Canadian government under Prime Minister Brian Mulroney tried to bring Quebec into the Constitution with the Meech Lake Accord which met Quebec's five minimum demands for more powers (which were recognition as a "distinct society", a constitutional veto; a restriction on federal spending power in areas of provincial jurisdiction, greater power over immigration; and a voice in choosing Supreme Court Judges). English Canadians' widespread opposition to the Meech Lake accord and Manitoba's and Newfoundland's failure to ratify the accord by the 23

June 1990 deadline after being let off the hook by Elijah Harper's filibuster left Quebec feeling badly rejected.

Emotions ran very high across Canada in the aftermath of Meech Lake. English Canadians were clearly in no mood to make concessions to Quebec. The steady rise of the Reform Party in the polls is a good barometer of English Canadian alienation.

Quebeckers were very angry and support for sovereignty soared (two-thirds of all Quebeckers and three-quarters of French-speaking Quebeckers were in favour of sovereignty according to a November 1990 poll[1]). A block of Quebec Members of Parliament split off from the governing Progressive Conservatives to work for Quebec sovereignty from within the federal government. It now tops the polls in Quebec and its leader, Lucien Bouchard, is the most popular Quebec politician.

The Liberal Quebec government of Premier Robert Bourassa, faces a strong separatist Parti Québécois opposition and counts many supporters of sovereignty among its members. True to form, Bourassa displayed his legendary ability to gauge the direction of the wind and avoid being blown over when he established the Bélanger-Campeau Commission on Quebec's Constitutional and Political Future last summer. At a minimum, the commission bought him some much-needed time: sovereigntists could blow off steam and their spirits could wane as memories of Meech Lake dimmed.

The Bélanger-Campeau Commission heard from an almost unbroken string of witnesses advocating sovereignty. Even business groups such as the Quebec Chamber of Commerce, who could be expected to have a better appreciation of the high economic stakes at risk, added their voice to the growing clamour in favour of sovereignty.

The sovereigntist bandwagon gained more momentum with the release of the Liberal party's Allaire report in late January (Constitutional Committee of the Liberal Party of Quebec, 1991). The Allaire report, which, surprisingly, was made less sovereigntist by Premier Bourassa before publication, calls for the transfer of eleven powers to Quebec, giving Quebec exclusive jurisdiction over 22 areas covering most of Quebec and leaving the federal government power over only four areas—defence and territorial security, customs and tariffs, currency and common debt, and equalization. It is, in effect, a proposal for sovereignty-association disguised as federalism. Worse still, in its recommendations for the referendum to be held before the fall of 1992, the Allaire report's expectations are clear: no agreement will be reached with the rest of Canada and the referendum will be on sovereignty.

The Allaire report played the same role in English Canada that the failure of Meech Lake did in Quebec. It made everyone angry.

The Allaire report was approved by the Quebec Liberal party's convention of March 8 to 10. Claude Ryan and his federalist supporters made a last ditch effort to have the Allaire proposals softened, but they were reportedly not even given the floor by the militant sovereigntists who dominated the convention.

Premier Bourassa appeased an angry Ryan and prevented a split in the party by saying that his first choice was to stay in Canada and that the Allaire report represented a negotiating position. This speech may have kept the Liberal party together, but it did little to placate the hostility stirred up in English Canada by the Allaire report.

After much behind the scenes inter-familial bickering, the Bélanger-Campeau Commission reported on schedule on March 28. In a report signed by 32 of 36 commissioners, the commission recommended that the Quebec government entertain binding offers of renewed federalism and that a law be passed requiring a referendum on sovereignty be held either between June 8 and 20, 1992, or between October 12 and 26, 1992 (Commission on the Political and Constitutional Future of Quebec, 1991a). Bélanger-Campeau also called for the establishment of two parliamentary committees—one to study the offers from the rest of Canada and the other to examine the impact of sovereignty. The commission provided no recommendations on what might constitute an acceptable offer. A yes vote on the referendum would lead to Quebec becoming a sovereign state one year later.

The Bélanger-Campeau's referendum deadlines have been passed into law by the Quebec National Assembly—but only after the agreement between the Liberal party and the Parti Québécois over the terms of the referendum broke down, causing the Parti Québécois to vote against the bill. The main bone of contention was that the Quebec government reserved the right to bypass the referendum on sovereignty if it would be in the best interest of Quebec.

The Bélanger-Campeau report and process has been greeted with suspicion and some hostility in the rest of Canada. The timetable is regarded as impossibly short. The refusal of Quebec to participate in constitutional meetings with the federal government and the rest of the provinces will make the process more difficult in some respects, but it will also give Quebec more flexibility in accepting an offer. This is important because it can prevent a potential catastrophe—another perceived rejection of Quebec demands, such as Meech Lake. The Quebec government's apparent refusal to be hamstrung by its own process is encouraging. Where there is a will to work out a deal, a way can be found.

The federal government response

The Canadian government has been working to try to defuse the emerging crisis. Prime Minister Mulroney gave two hard-hitting speeches in Toronto and Quebec in mid-February to counter growing support for Quebec sovereignty. The sovereignty issue is not easy for the Prime Minister to handle. He himself came to power from a Quebec base. Some of his key Quebec ministers and many Quebeckers in his Conservative parliamentary caucus could switch to the sovereigntist side if an acceptable offer for renewed federalism is not forthcoming. Outside Quebec, there is the perception that the Mulroney government has favoured Quebec. The popularity of his Progressive Conservative party is at the dismally low level of 15 percent in the polls, well behind the two main opposition parties.[2] This makes the Prime Minister's job all the more difficult.

The Prime Minister has taken initiatives to respond to the emerging crisis. The Citizens' Forum on Canada's Future was established under the chairmanship of Keith Spicer to canvass the views of Canadians. A parliamentary committee, chaired jointly by Conservative MP James Edwards and Senator Gérald Beaudoin, was set up to examine the formula for amending the Constitution. The unanimity requirement for certain changes in the Constitution is seen as being an important stumbling block that led to the Meech Lake debacle. Both the Citizens' Forum and the parliamentary committee on the amending formula reported in late June.

The Beaudoin-Edwards Committee recommended the so-called Victoria amending formula with four regional vetoes for matters dealing with the Queen, minority languages, and provincial proprietary rights over their resources. The committee also called for a two-year time limit for ratification as opposed to the current three-year limit and for an optional referendum to confirm a consensus or to influence recalcitrant provincial governments. The report endorsed the politicians-only approach to constitution making that the federal government was already pursuing (Delacourt, 1991, p.A4).

In its final report, the Citizens' Forum reviewed what it heard from the people of Canada (1991b). Its most important contribution was to articulate the views of Canadians, particularly English Canadians, on the key issues facing the country. Its recommendations were relatively few. National institutions and symbols should be reviewed to give them more importance. A simple elegant preamble on Canada should be added to the Constitution. Quebec should have the freedom to be itself—a unique society. The official languages policy should be independently reviewed. Funding for multiculturalism should be eliminated. There should be a fair settlement of native land claims and there should be native self-government. A high priority should be attached to eliminating overlapping government jurisdictions and programs, and government efficiency should be identified as a major goal by placing programs as close as possible to the people. The Senate should be either fundamentally reformed or abolished.

In April the prime minister reshuffled the cabinet and named Joe Clark as Constitutional Affairs Minister heading up a cabinet committee on national unity with a mandate to come up with proposals that will resolve the constitutional impasse. The new constitutional proposals will be referred to a new joint Commons-Senate committee in September. The committee is charged to consult with Canadians and to report by February 1992. This leaves little time for securing provincial approval of the proposal before submitting it to Quebec. The federal government apparently does not intend to be bound by Quebec's time schedule.

Keeping Canada together

There are two things which could help to keep the country together. First, recognition by Quebeckers of the very heavy economic costs of sovereignty. This could serve to bring the soaring independentist spirits of the more nationalistic Quebeckers back down to earth. There is also hope that time will heal Quebec's wounded pride over Meech Lake and that the emotion-driven support in Quebec for sovereignty will wane. A poll conducted in April which showed that support for sovereignty had receded to 48 percent is encouraging.[3]

Second, Canadians outside Quebec must realize that it is necessary to make some compromises to keep the country together. One hopes that Canadians can be persuaded to go further than Meech Lake—if they can be assured that the proposed constitutional changes will satisfy Quebec as more than a stopgap, and if they can see that there are high economic costs for the rest of Canada if Quebec separates. There is a trade-off of reduced potential costs for compromises made.

Keeping the country together will not be easy and it will require much goodwill and sacrifices on both sides. The Quebec government's acceptance of the Allaire report's demands to accept offers from the rest of Canada will make it difficult to reach an agreement. Given the response of English Canada to the relatively minor devolution of powers proposed under the Meech Lake accord, concessions to Quebec will not be easily granted. A recent poll indicated that three quarters of English Canadians were willing to take the risk that Quebec would separate rather than give in to its demands for more powers.[4]

As a result of Meech Lake, Quebeckers have lost their patience with the process of constitutional change. The Quebec government has indicated its unwillingness to go back to the bargaining table with the federal and provincial governments as required by the current process for amending the Constitution. Since the federal government does not have the power to restructure Confederation as a result of bilateral negotiations with Quebec, there is a danger that Quebec might get frustrated and decide to proceed unilaterally and to seek constitutional ratification after the fact. The Parti Québécois, which is currently leading the Quebec Liberals in the polls by a significant margin and will gain additional support if the Liberal Quebec government is unable to negotiate a devolution of powers or lead the province to sovereignty, is itself on record as favouring a unilateral declaration of independence following a referendum on the issue (Parti Québécois, 1990,p.3). A UDI would be very dangerous and could lead to confrontation with unpredictable but likely disastrous consequences.

The constitutional future of a Canada without Quebec

What would happen to the rest of Canada if Quebec were to separate? The interim and final reports of the Citizens' Forum have revealed that Canadians outside Quebec are developing a different vision of the country than Quebeckers are (Citizens' Forum, 1991a 1991b).

According to the Citizens' Forum, most Canadians outside Quebec do not believe in provinces or regions "going their own way" without regard to the effects on the rest of Canada. A core of common values was identified. Encouragingly, the economy is the most often mentioned among leading issues facing Canada. The federal government is regarded as the chosen instrument for directing the economy, but this view is tempered by a healthy scepticism and recognition that government policies have severely eroded Canada's economy and government intervention must be reduced. The federal government's role should be to set national standards in health and education, to maintain national symbols, to conduct international affairs, and to manage the economy, including regional equalization. Canadians strongly reject the decentralization of the Meech Lake accord. They strongly support the equality of provinces but not the concept of "two founding peoples". Official bilingualism and multiculturalism are also out of favour. But they support Senate reform, native rights, and empowerment to make governments more responsive to the public.

The majority canvassed would accept Quebec separation in order to avoid inequality among the provinces, preferential treatment for Quebec, or damage to Canada's capacity to address national issues. Support for western separation is negligible. These predominant views provide a favourable climate for a successful round of constitutional negotiations dealing with issues such as Senate reform and native rights. But they offer less encouragement for a compromise involving decentralization or special status that would be required to keep Quebec in Canada.

The current constitutional crisis is very serious. It is very likely that Quebec will not receive an acceptable binding constitutional proposal from the rest of Canada in time to avoid the October 1992 referendum deadline. Given the current volatile state of public opinion in Quebec and the possibility of another affront to Quebec's national pride, a referendum in Quebec could easily result in a vote for Quebec sovereignty. If Premier Bourassa somehow manages to avoid a referendum and thwart sovereigntists, there is a risk that this would help the PQ to win the next provincial election, which must be held by 1994. Strong forces are in play that could lead to Quebec's separation one way or another if a new constitutional deal is not reached.

What would be likely to happen to the rest of Canada if Quebec were to separate? With or without Quebec a round of constitutional reform is underway that will result in a new Canada. The reports of the Citizens' Forum give a good indication of where this round is headed. It will likely preserve a strong federal system. It will probably include some constitutional reforms such as a Triple-E Senate to satisfy the west (interpreting the equal E to mean more equal). It will also focus on aboriginal and other issues that were put on the back-burner during the Quebec round. Without Quebec, Canada would be a more homogeneous country politically and hence more governable. But it would also be a weaker and less interesting country. The key problem facing the country must be reconciling the English Canadian vision of Canada identified by the Citizens' Forum with Quebec's vision.

The pressing need to understand the economic consequences of Quebec sovereignty

Quebec is not gone yet. A careful assessment of the economic consequences of Quebec sovereignty can make a difference in the debate over the political and economic future of Canada and Quebec. And, if worse comes to worst and Quebec separates, an economic assessment is imperative to prepare for the disruptions in store. It is in a spirit of hope that this study is offered, but also with a realization that it should still prove useful if our dreams of a unified Canada are shattered.

A roadmap for the book

Chapter 2 of this study provides a review of the pre-Bélanger-Campeau literature dealing with the economic consequences of Quebec sovereignty. Chapter 3 presents a detailed critique of the economic studies done for the Bélanger-Campeau Commission. Because of the great importance of the studies for the debate on Quebec sovereignty and because of their unavailability in English, the studies are summarized for the benefit of anglophone audiences. Chapter 4 reviews the evidence on the economic viability of a sovereign Quebec by focusing on the available statistical data. Finally, Chapter 5 offers my conclusions on the economic consequences of a sovereign Quebec.

Notes

1. Poll conducted November 14-19 for the Toronto Star, CTV and La Presse by the Environics Research Group and published on Canada Press Newswire November 26, 1990.

2. Results of an Angus Reid-Southam Poll conducted April 25-May 7 reported in Julian Beltrame, "In from the fringe, Poll shows Reform, Bloc support surging," *Ottawa Citizen*, May 13, 1991, p.A1.

3. "Sovereignty support cooling: poll," *Ottawa Citizen*, May 1, 1991.

4. Results of a Gallup poll cited in Angus Reid (1991, p.A1).

Chapter 2

What Others Have Said

Introduction

A CONSENSUS ON THE ECONOMIC IMPACT of Quebec sovereignty has emerged in Quebec. It was articulated by a group of prominent Quebec economists speaking before the Bélanger-Campeau Commission on behalf of the Association des Économistes Québécois (1990). If Quebec were to separate, they argue, there would be no significant impact in the long run on the Quebec economy and that the short-run impact would depend very much on how the break was made. The smoother and more harmonious the political and economic relations between Quebec and Canada during the split, the smaller the economic disruptions would be. Uncertainty during the transition period is seen as being the only cost of sovereignty.

This chapter reviews the pre-Bélanger-Campeau-report literature on the economic consequences of Quebec sovereignty to see if the literature supports this emerging consensus. Subject to a few exceptions, this chapter focuses only on the more rigorous technical analyses of sovereignty, which have been relatively rare, and does not cover the journalistic and partisan articles and papers dealing with sovereignty. The exceptions concern papers which have been widely quoted in the debate over Quebec sovereignty or which deal with important issues not covered in analytical papers.

The chapter is divided into sections, each treating a specific type of analysis. The second section addresses the critical question of the surplus from Confederation. The larger the surplus, the greater the gains are from membership in the Canadian federation. The third section covers general equilibrium analyses which seek to estimate the overall impact of Quebec sovereignty on the output and income of Quebec and other regions. The fourth section deals with fiscal balance studies which concentrate narrowly on the federal deficit or surplus with Quebec and the other regions; it attempts to show who gains and who loses from Confederation. Fiscal balance studies have been a perennial favourite of Canadian analysts. The fifth section focuses on studies of the trade flows between Quebec and the rest of Canada. The sixth section examines some studies which have been prepared by financial institutions and have been used particularly by the Parti Québécois to show the economic viability of a sovereign Quebec. The seventh section looks at the question of the viability of a Quebec dollar. The eighth section considers the issue of financing government deficits and debt. The ninth section reviews the evidence on the likely effect of constitutional uncertainties on the Quebec and Canadian economies. The tenth section provides conclusions on the literature review.

The scarcity of up-to-date hard analysis of the costs and benefits of Confederation and the economic impact of Quebec sovereignty is cause for concern. Important decisions on the future of Quebec and Canada that are currently being made without adequate information on their likely economic consequences.

The surplus from Confederation

The most important economic argument in favour of a federation has to be that economic integration of the component parts creates a surplus which can be distributed among the participants. In the final overview study for the C.D. Howe Accent Quebec series, Judith Maxwell and Caroline Pestieau list four ways to generate the surplus:

- The opportunity to achieve greater scale and specialization in economic activity can lead to gains from trade among the

participants in the form of more efficient production and higher incomes.
- Interregional compensation and insurance programs for pooling the risks of cyclical fluctuations (both short- and long-term) can produce a smoother flow of economic activity and create a more favourable environment for development within each region.
- The sharing of such joint services as transportation, communications, and defence can lead to both cost savings and an improvement in the quantity and quality of these services.
- Bargaining power in international negotiations can be increased through the consolidation of strength (Maxwell and Pestieau, 1980, p.14).

After reviewing the Canadian experience in generating a surplus in each of these four ways, namely gains from trade, pooling of risk, sharing of overheads, and international bargaining power, Maxwell and Pestieau express some doubts about the size of surplus which has actually accrued.

> In summary, the current perceptions of the surplus from the existing system are not particularly favourable. In areas where surpluses have been created as a result of specialization in interprovincial trade, most provinces are now seeking ways to restructure their economies in the direction of less specialization. In areas where the pooling of risks or sharing of overheads could be expected to generate a surplus, several provinces object strongly to both the methods employed and the results achieved. Finally, in areas where a consolidation of strength could be expected to increase Canadian bargaining power, certain analysts would argue that this power has not been used to create a healthy national economy, let alone a surplus for the individual regions. (Maxwell and Pestieau, 1980, pp.20-21)

In their pioneering study of regional aspects of Confederation Whalley and Trela used general equilibrium analysis of the gains and losses from Confederation and concluded that "Confederation may be the source of a deficit rather than a surplus" (Whalley and Trela, 1986, p.196). But these results derive largely from the distortions in resource allocation caused by the National Energy Program. Consequently, their study may not still be applicable. They also voice some pessimism about the prospects for future surplus as a result of the tendency towards regional balkanization and the competitiveness of the Canadian economy in international transactions (1980, p.21).

The strongest argument in favour of federalism advanced by Maxwell and Pestieau is that the regions together in a united Canada have more bargaining power in dealing with their main trading partners than they would have if they were divided into smaller groups (1980, p.23). Subsequent events have borne this out. In negotiating the free trade deal with the United States, which is considered to be so important to Quebec in reducing its dependence on the Canadian market, Canada made two important concessions: guarantee of access to Canadian energy and the modifications to the auto-pact. These concessions could not have been made by a sovereign Quebec.

Regarding the surplus, the Task Force on Canadian Unity argues that "it says something in favour of the present economic union that the Parti Québécois would like to retain many of its elements" (1979, p.76). This is still true today, but perhaps less so. The task force also noted that "there is simply no evidence to support the contention that Quebec has been or is getting more than a fair share of the surplus generated by the Canadian economic union" (1979, p.76).

Recently, Quebec business leaders, such as those represented by the Chamber of Commerce (1990, pp.11-17), have expressed scepticism before the Bélanger-Campeau Commission about the surplus from Confederation. This stems from their dissatisfaction with what they perceive to be a mismanagement of fiscal and monetary policy. Many Quebec businesspeople believe that the federal deficit is out of control and that high interest rates are driving up the Canadian dollar and undermining the competitiveness of Canadian industry.

In my view, existing studies substantially underestimate the surplus from Confederation. If the surplus were not large, how could real income per capita in Canada be the second highest in the world behind the United States as it currently is? Additional evidence that the surplus is probably considerable is provided by the estimates of the output gains resulting from free trade with the United States, which were reported by the Department of Finance to be from 2.5 to 8.9 percent with most estimates around 3 percent (1988, p.32).

General equilibrium analysis

In a report prepared for the Macdonald Commission, the most comprehensive and thorough study ever of the regional costs and benefits of Confederation, John Whalley and Irene Trela evaluated the regional impacts of the more important government policies within a broader framework than the fiscal accounts (1986). The policies considered included the federal tariff, transport subsidies, energy policies, intergovernmental transfers, provincial impediments to goods and factor flows, the federal tax system, federal transfers to persons, non-tariff trade policies, regional development policies, and agricultural policies.

Whalley and Trela used a 1981 micro-consistent interregional data set for Canada which records production, demand, and interregional and international trade in combination with data on the policy elements. They performed counterfactual analysis using this data set for various changes in policies, using both partial equilibrium and general equilibrium techniques. Their general equilibrium model was calibrated to the data for the 1981 benchmark year, assuming that the interregional economy was in an equilibrium situation that year.

A general equilibrium model is basically a Walrasian system where prices are determined by the equilibrium of supply and demand in the relevant market. In the model used by Whalley and Trela, demand for final goods in each region is treated as the outcome of utility maximization, with each region maximizing a six-level nested constant elasticity of substitution (CES)/linear expenditure system (LES) utility function subject to its regional budget constraint. The regional budget constraint includes capital, labour and resource income received by residents, along with intergovernmental transfers and transfers to persons from the federal government. Supply of goods and services and demand for factors in each region are determined by profit maximization based on production functions with assumed parameters. Demand for intermediate inputs and for factors of production is based on cost minimization. Imports are other sources of supply. Taxes and subsidies are wedges between supply and demand prices. Various other policies are treated as *ad valorem* tariff equivalents. Increasing returns to scale can be incorporated in the model as a variant.

In addition to equilibrium conditions for supply and demand in goods and factor markets in the model, there are other equilibrium conditions of budget balance at both the federal and regional government levels and of external balance as well as the imposition of zero profit conditions imposed on all industries in all regions and abroad.

Six regions are identified in the model—Atlantic Canada, Quebec, Ontario, Manitoba and Saskatchewan, Alberta, and British Columbia. Two levels of aggregation are used, one with six goods produced by each region, and one with thirteen. These six goods can be assumed to be qualitatively different both interregionally and internationally (the Armington assumption). Public goods are treated separately. There are three types of factors of production: capital services, labour services, and resources. Capital is generally assumed to be mobile. Labour is assumed mobile across sectors and partially mobile across regions, but immobile internationally. Resources are assumed to be immobile. Other assumptions depend on the model variant utilized.

Analysis of the impact of policies is conducted by altering one or more policies and determining the new equilibrium in the model. There will be related changes in resource allocation, relative prices, and the distribution of income both within and across provinces.

The results of a simulation in which each of the regions is assumed to withdraw from the Confederation are shown in table 1. In conducting the simulations, it is assumed that on withdrawal federal taxes are not collected from the region, that federal expenditures including intergovernmental transfers and transfers to persons in the region are not made, and that labour is immobile between the withdrawing region and the remainder of the country. The results show that if Quebec were to withdraw, it would be worse off by $6.4 billion and the five remaining regions would be better off by $3.2 billion. Atlantic Canada would also be a big loser if it were to withdraw. Alberta would gain the most from leaving Confederation would be Alberta because of the energy rents Alberta would regain. But Ontario, British Columbia, and Manitoba and Saskatchewan would also gain. The most important policies producing the pattern of gains and losses are energy policy, equalization, and the tariff. Of these, energy policy is by far the most important.

There are many problems with estimates from general equilibrium models. The parameters are generally not estimated empirically; instead, they are calibrated based on earlier studies. For regional trade elasticities, this is a real problem because there are no time series data and no earlier studies. Also the assumptions that equilibrium is achieved and markets function perfectly are rather strict. In addition, general equilibrium models provide comparative static results and do not capture dynamic impacts. All these criticisms can be applied to the Whalley and Trela study. The obvious reply, however, is that it is necessary to take this approach and make these types of assumptions to get any estimates at all and that alternative approaches are not available. Whalley and Trela's study is clearly pioneering: no one has ever before been able to make such estimates.

The most obvious problem with Whalley and Trela's estimates of the impact of various regions withdrawing from Confederation, a problem which they acknowledge, is that their data apply to policies in effect

TABLE 1

GENERAL EQUILIBRIUM IMPACTS OF WITHDRAWAL FROM CONFEDERATION BY INDIVIDUAL REGIONS, USING 1981 DATA

(Hicksian EV's in $ Millions)

			Withdrawal by			
Impacts on	Atlantic	Quebec	Ontario	Manitoba /Sask.	Alberta	B.C
Atlantic Canada	-5,150	358	-512	-189	-1,417	-329
Quebec	607	-6,394	-1,937	-663	-5,674	-1,197
Ontario	792	1,801	713	-1,204	-7,901	-1,943
Manitoba/Saskatchewan	168	331	-630	1,310	-2,209	-429
Alberta	124	308	-1,154	-751	20,534	-667
British Columbia	208	419	-1,163	-385	-2,875	2,389
Total for six original regions	-3,251	-3,177	-4,683	-1,882	459	-2,176
Total for five remaining regions	1,899	3,217	-5,396	-3,192	-20,076	-4,565

Note: Each of these model experiments is specified by removing intergovernmental transfers and federal transfers from to persons in the region, federal taxes paid, and expenditures by the federal government on goods produced by the region. Any gain or loss to the federal government produced by the model has been reallocated to the remaining regions on a proportional basis.

Source: Whalley and Trela (1986, p.198).

in 1981. Three very important policy changes after 1981 which are not accounted for in their analysis are the termination of the National Energy Program, the inauguration of the Canada-U.S. Free Trade Agreement, and tax reform, including the Goods and Services Tax. The National Energy Program in particular had a very substantial regional impact, favouring other regions at the expense of Alberta and, to a lesser extent, British Columbia and Saskatchewan. According to Whalley and Trela, energy policy by far dominates the regional effects produced by other policies. The Economic Council of Canada is updating Whalley and Trela's analysis as part of the research program leading up to its 1991 annual review. Their research should help us better understand how recent changes in policies and economic developments have helped change the distribution of benefits and costs of Confederation.

Fiscal balance studies

One very partial measure of the costs and benefits of Confederation is given by the federal government fiscal balance by province. Based on certain assumptions about the incidence of federal government revenues and expenditures, this provides an estimate of how much money the federal government injects into or withdraws from a region. It does not show anything about the likely second and subsequent round impacts of respending the money. It also does not adequately quantify the impact of regulatory or commercial policies.

John Whalley and Irene Trela have underlined additional problems with the balance sheet approach (1986, pp.182-183). The first is how to deal with interregional labour mobility. If labour is perfectly mobile, it is not possible to associate a particular group of people with a region. For instance, should a region's gain from a policy be associated with the gain of the people there before the policy was introduced or with those there afterwards. The second is the problem of interregional asset ownership. As there are no data on interregional asset ownership, it is impossible to allocate gains and losses associated with the ownership of assets to the appropriate regions in which the assets are owned. The third is the implicit zero sum game assumption that what one region gains another must lose. But there can be either a surplus or deadweight loss resulting from Confederation. The fourth is that fiscal balance sheet exercises do not spell out the alternatives which are being compared to the existing arrangements.

All the caveats notwithstanding, fiscal balance sheet exercises became very popular after the Parti Québécois came to power in 1976 and after the release of the new provincial accounts which made such calculations possible. At that time a public controversy broke out between the federal and Quebec governments over whether the federal government fiscal balance with Quebec was a deficit or a surplus. The answer depended quite critically on the assumptions made to distribute federal revenues and expenditures across provinces. The Quebec government jumped the gun and published provincial economic data for Quebec which basically used the same incidence assumptions made by Statistics Canada in preparing the data (the Quebec government and Statistics Canada cooperated in preparing the provincial economic accounts, see Quebec, Ministry of Industry and Commerce 1977). The federal Minister of Finance countered with a more reasonable statement which made a persuasive case for the use of alternative assumptions (1977). Using the new fiscal balance data, the Economic Council of Canada calculated the likely short-term changes in both the level and distribution of taxes if provinces were to become fiscally autonomous (Glynn, 1978).

In 1979, on the basis of its own examination of the fiscal balance data, the Task Force on Canadian Unity concluded thus:

> Statistical evidence from recently developed provincial accounts fails to establish that Quebec has been a major net recipient of federal funds (that is federal expenditures minus tax contributions from Quebec) until quite recently, when temporary subsidies for oil imports were established. Moreover, the evidence confirms in part the current contention that central government expenditures have been concentrated in income support measures, while the province has been receiving a disproportionately small portion of funds to generate employment. (1979, p. 75)

More recently, Robert L. Mansell and Ronald C. Schlenker have prepared an analysis of the regional distribution of federal fiscal balances following an updated version of the Department of Finance's methodology (1977). The adjustments to the provincial economic accounts data for this purpose are three. First, certain indirect taxes are reallocated to reflect the province in which the good is consumed rather than produced, reflecting the generally accepted regional incidence of such taxes. Second, public debt interest payments to non-Canadians were removed from the public debt charges which are distributed across provinces. Third, transfers associated with regulated pricing of energy were included (under the National Energy Program, when the gap between the international and domestic price widened, these transfers became very large). An additional adjustment was made to allow for the increasing federal deficits from the mid-1970s and the pattern of increasingly negative fiscal contributions. The adjustment was made by increasing revenues for each province by the same percentage so that the aggregate revenue of all provinces would equal total expenditures in each year and the federal budget position would be in balance. All nominal magnitudes are expressed in 1990 dollars. No adjustments are made for the fact that departments are headquartered in Ottawa.

Table 2 from Mansell and Schlenker shows the provincial allocation of net federal fiscal balances after making all the above-noted adjustments, and table 3 provides the same data in per capita form. From 1961 to 1988, Quebec received by far the largest federal fiscal contribution ($72.4 billion), but on a per capita basis the federal fiscal contribution to Quebec ($401) was much smaller than that to the Atlantic provinces or Manitoba. Alberta made by far the largest contribution to the federal government from 1961 to 1988 ($207.6 billion). The large federal fiscal contribution to Quebec at the beginning of the 1980s reflected in large part the subsidies for the consumption of petroleum out of the petroleum compensation account. During the 1980s, Quebec's gain in fiscal transactions with the federal government turned into a small loss by 1988.

André Raynauld has also calculated the federal fiscal balance from 1961 to 1988 (1990, pp.20-31). His results differ from those of Mansell and Schlenker in that he did not make all of the adjustments they made, except for distributing the deficit based on tax revenues. He also did not denominate all fiscal balances in constant 1990 dollars.

In addition, Raynauld made another adjustment to public debt charges which Mansell and Schlenker did not make. The previous adjustment for the deficit implies that the debt is eliminated, he argues, so the distribution of public debt charges loses its significance. Raynauld proposes two alternative adjustments for public debt charges. Because spending could be higher, without public debt charges, the first adjustment spreads public debt charges among provinces based on the distribution of other expenditures. The second adjustment distributes public debt charges based on tax revenues on the assumption that taxes could be reduced. Raynauld argues that such an adjustment is all the more necessary because the payments of interest on the public debt result from voluntary investment choices by citizens. Quebec residents receive only 18 percent of the interest on the public debt, while Ontario residents receive 61 percent because of the decisions they make to purchase federal government obligations. In my view, Raynauld's case for this adjustment is convincing.

These adjustments to the distribution of public debt charges are very significant. The net federal balance in Quebec calculated by Raynauld is a surplus of $987 million in Quebec before the adjustments. But after a $2,029 million adjustment to expenditures, there would be a deficit of $1,042 million, and after a $1,776 million adjustment to taxes, there would be a $789 million deficit. Depending on the method of adjustment chosen, Quebec realized a gain of between $800 million and more that $1 billion in 1988 as a result of its fiscal transactions with the federal government.

Raynauld's estimates of the net fiscal balance with Quebec from 1961 to 1988 are given in table 4. During the 1960s, after making the first kind of adjustment to public debt charges of spreading across provinces based on expenditures, Quebec experienced a cumulative net fiscal loss of $4.6 billion in its relations with the federal government. But, after 1972, Quebec began to gain. From 1972 to 1980, Quebec experienced a cumulative net fiscal benefit of $12.3 billion, which increased to $22.7 billion from 1981 to 1985. From 1986 to 1988 Quebec continued to register a moderate gain in the $1 to $1.7 billion range. Since 1972, Quebec's fiscal benefit has averaged $2.3 billion per year. Quebec has clearly gained from its fiscal relations with the federal government based on Raynauld's estimates. Similar results are shown in table 4 if the second type of adjustment to public debt charges (distributing based on revenues) is made.

Isabella D. Horry and Michael Walker of the Fraser Institute have also done a study of the provincial distribution of federal revenues and expenditures (1991). Their study differs from those of Mansell and Schlenker and of Raynauld in that they use data from the Financial Management System rather than the Provincial Economic Accounts. The Financial Management System is a standard system of public accounting developed by Statistics Canada. Their study does not make any of the adjustments made by Mansell and Schlenker and by Raynauld, except for an adjustment to eliminate the deficit. Indirect taxes are distributed based on factor incomes rather than on consumption, thereby allocating the taxes disproportionately to Ontario and Quebec, where manufacturing is concentrated. Horry and Walker show that Quebec derives a net benefit in 1988 of $1,996 million from its fiscal relations with the federal government. In per capita terms at $304, Quebec's net fiscal benefit is only a fraction of those received in Saskatchewan at $1,854, Manitoba at $1,521, New Brunswick at $2,526 and Prince Edward Island at $4,315. Ontario, British Columbia, and especially Alberta are net losers in their fiscal transactions with the federal government. Ontario's net loss is $831 per capita; British Columbia's is $645; and Alberta's is $1,688. In my view, by allocating indirect taxes based on factor incomes instead of the more generally accepted consumer expenditures and by failing to adjust for the distribution of public debt charges, Horry and Walker open their estimates of net fiscal benefits to some criticism.

A more reliable estimate of Quebec's gain in its fiscal relations with the federal government than Mansell and Schlenker's, Raynauld's, or Horry and Walker's would require that all the adjustments suggested by Mansell and Schlenker be made to the data as well as the additional adjustment to public debt charges proposed by Raynauld. In addition, with respect to the Mansell and Schlenker and Raynauld estimates, part of the net federal balance outside of the country should be allocated to Quebec to reflect the benefits Quebec derives from foreign aid, defence and other expenditures abroad. The federal net balance outside the country was estimated by Mansell and Schlenker to be $8.8 billion (1990 dollars) in 1988. Quebec's share, based on its 25.6 percent population share in 1988, would be more than $2.2 billion or $339 per capita, a far from trivial sum. In the absence of all the required adjustments, all estimates significantly underestimate Quebec's gain from its fiscal relations with the federal government. If estimated correctly, Quebec's gain would be substantial.

Static fiscal balance calculations may be misleading if it would be possible to achieve economies after separation. For instance, the Quebec Chamber of Commerce argued in its brief to the Bélanger-Campeau Commission that spending is inflated by overlapping jurisdictions and by duplication between the federal and provincial governments (1990, p.13). The only concrete evidence cited is a study done twelve years ago by Germain Julien and Marcel Proulx at École Nationale d'Administration Publique. According to this study, 277 of 465 programs examined, or 60 percent, involved some degree of overlap (1978, p.33). Overlap occurred in all sectors except the post office, defence, and veterans affairs. The elimination of overlap is expected by Julien and Proulx to provide more than a billion dollars in savings for a sovereign Quebec. Their estimate overstates the potential savings since the degree of overlap has been reduced by federal government expenditure restraint in recent years.

Trade flows

There are no current comprehensive studies of trade flows between Canada and Quebec. Indeed, the data on interprovincial trade flows are not available in constant dollar terms, and their coverage outside the manufacturing sector is poor.

Prior to the Bélanger-Campeau Commission, the most recent thorough study of trade flows between Canada and Quebec was carried out by the Canadian Unity Information Office in 1978; their study dealt with trade flows in 1967 and changes in trade flows between 1967 and 1974. The study, which presents disaggregated data on trade flows by industry, highlighted the extent to which the industrial structure of Quebec was concentrated in industries related to forest products (wood, furniture, and pulp and paper) and in those non-durable, labour-intensive consumer goods (leather, textiles, knitting mills and clothing). Of the $1.2 billion trade surplus with the rest of Canada which Quebec enjoyed in 1974, $1 billion was concentrated in "soft" industries (textiles, knitting, leather, clothing, furniture) which are highly protected by tariffs and are increasingly subject to foreign competition. These "soft"

TABLE 2

TOTAL FEDERAL FISCAL BALANCES BY REGION WITH BALANCED FEDERAL BUDGET
(Millions of Dollars)

	NFLD	PEI	NS	NB	QUE	ONT	MAN	SASK	ALTA	BC	TERR	Sum	Outside
1961	-380	-124	-1,054	-559	1,345	2,317	-284	-535	221	346	-267	1,026	-1,026
1961-1969	-4,681	-1,804	-11,783	-6045	6,726	24,412	-3,009	-3,048	3,944	9,093	-2,592	11,211	-11,211
1970-1979	-13,055	-4,028	-24,992	-15,052	-31,538	32,948	-5,966	-1,809	69,076	19,492	-3,723	20,353	-20,353
1980-1988	-18,477	-4,618	-28,657	-19,569	-47,629	46,972	-13,414	-2,790	134,562	17,577	-11,172	52,814	-52,814
TOTAL	-36,184	-10,450	-65,433	-40,665	-72,441	104,332	-22,389	-7,647	207,582	46,152	-17,487	84,378	-84,378
1986	-2,283	-491	-2,940	-1,917	-1,018	12,610	-1,282	-1,090	5,363	1,950	-1,719	7,384	-7,384
1987	-1,993	-469	-2,410	-1,754	8	13,473	-1,671	-2,227	4,006	2,405	-1,022	8,346	-8,346
1988	-1,969	-513	-2,444	-1,823	356	13,110	-1,824	-1,776	4,187	2,669	-1,168	8,805	-8,805

Source: Mansell and Schlenker (1990).

TABLE 3

PER CAPITA FEDERAL BALANCES BY REGION WITH BALANCED FEDERAL BUDGET ($1990)

	NFLD	PEI	NS	NB	QUE	ONT	MAN	SASK	ALTA	BC	TERR	Average
1961	-830	-1,180	-1,430	-935	256	372	-308	-579	166	212	-7,030	56
1961-1969	-1,061	-1,841	-1,729	-1,091	136	395	-349	-359	297	541	-6,819	63
1970-1979	-2,382	-3,451	-3,047	-2,256	-507	413	-687	-198	3,686	820	-6,071	90
1980-1988	-3,603	-4,102	-3,698	-3,089	-820	562	-1,416	-292	6,563	687	-16,855	233
AVERAGE	-2,350	-3,143	-2,833	-2,150	-401	455	-813	-280	3,521	688	-9,778	127
1986	-4,019	-3,865	-3,367	-2,700	-156	1,384	-1,010	-1,079	2,258	675	-22,621	291
1987	-3,508	-3,694	-2,745	-2,464	1	1,454	-1,549	-2,192	1,685	822	-13,270	326
1988	-3,466	-3,979	-2,768	-2,553	54	1,391	-1,683	-1,753	1,748	894	-15,167	340

Source: Mansell and Schlenker (1990).

TABLE 4

**NET FISCAL BALANCE OF FEDERAL GOVERNMENT
IN QUEBEC, 1961-88
(- Federal Surplus/+ Federal Deficit)**

	Method 1			Method 2	
	$	$		$	$
	Millions	Per Capita		Millions	Per Capita
1961-71	-4,575			-4,020	
1972-80	12,268			10,640	
1981-85	22,705			18,282	
1986	1,716	262		1,326	203
1987	1,392	211		1,075	163
1988	1,042	157		789	119

Method 1: Net fiscal balance after correction for the federal deficit, public debt charges being allocated to other expenditure programs and distributed among the provinces based on total expenditures.

Method 2: Net fiscal balance after correction for the federal deficit, public debt charges serving to reduce taxes and being distributed among the provinces based on total taxes paid.

Source: Raynauld (1990).

industries accounted for 18 percent of Quebec's manufacturing shipments and nearly 30 percent of the province's employment in manufacturing in 1974. The average level of tariff protection in Quebec based on the structure of Quebec production was estimated to be 10 percent in 1974, or 1.5 to 2 percentage points higher than in any of the other Canadian regions. It would be useful to have more current information on industrial structure, trade flows, and effective tariff rates.

In another study done for the Canadian Unity Information Office in 1979 on the special problems of the textile and clothing industry, the structure of the industry and interregional trade flows were examined. In 1976, two hundred thousand people were employed in the textile industry in Quebec, with total wages and salaries of approximately $2 billion. Textile and clothing industry employment accounted for 23 percent of employment in Quebec manufacturing. In 1976, almost 60 percent of employment and 62 percent of establishments in the industry were in Quebec compared to 31 and 27 percent respectively in Ontario.

The study concluded that Canadian consumers bear the cost of protection of this industry, and Quebec benefits from it.

An early attempt to model the economic impact of Quebec separation on trade flows was by Tim Hazledine (1978). He used an *ad hoc* five-region Canadian economic model which combined production, trade flows, employment, and incomes. The model was calibrated using 1974 data. Hazledine estimated that if the Canadian external tariff were applied to Quebec following separation, the cost to Quebec would be about 5 percent of Quebec GDP. Given the change in trade flows and the progress which has been made in modelling, Hazledine's analysis is primarily of historical interest and has little relevance to the current policy debate. Another study by L. Auer and K. Mills (1978), which was prepared for the same conference, also examined the impact of imposing Canadian tariffs on an independent Quebec using 1974 data. This study, which produced estimates of lost output and employment that were about half those of Hazledine, is also outdated. Finally, Leon Courville in his independent 1979 used the same data in his independent 1979 study to estimate losses of output which were very similar to those of Hazledine. A problem with all these studies—in addition to the obvious one of being out-of-date—is that they estimate only the short-run impact of the disruption of trade flows resulting from separation and the imposition of external tariffs. The long-run impact would be mitigated by the redeployment of capital and labour, which is not included in any of these models as it would be in a general equilibrium model.

The Task Force on Canadian Unity wrote the following in 1979:

> We have examined the evidence provided by a number of recent studies dealing with interregional trade, the interprovincial shipment of manufactured goods, the number of jobs dependent on the Canadian market, federal expenditures in Quebec, and other related topics. The major conclusion to be drawn from the trade data is that Quebec's economy is highly dependent upon the Canadian common market. Canada's tariff structure and trade policy have a major impact on the level of production, employment and income of that province's manufacturing sector. Compared with its international exports whose production takes relatively large inputs of natural resources and technology, Quebec's trade with Canada is based upon the manufacture of labour intensive products. It relies on Canadian markets for

the sale of about $7 billion of these goods, most of which could not withstand foreign competition. Severing the ties to Canada's customs union would profoundly disrupt Quebec's economy. Quebec's and Ontario's favourable trade balances with the rest of Canada unquestionably indicate that both provinces derive definite advantages from the Canadian customs union. (1979, p.75)

André Raynauld has prepared for the Association des Economistes Québécois and for the Conseil du Patronat du Québec an analysis of more recent trade flows that also underlines the high degree of interdependence of Canada and Quebec and particularly the dependence of Quebec on Canada (Raynauld, 1990, pp.13-19 and ASDEQ, 1990,pp.10-13). Unfortunately, this analysis contains no data on the structure of Quebec trade in manufactured goods. But the aggregate data presented confirms the conclusions of the earlier studies about the greater dependence of Quebec on exports to Canada than vice versa.

The regional distribution of trade in manufactured goods in 1984 as measured by manufacturers' shipments is shown in table 5 taken from Raynauld. It is striking the greater extent to which Quebec is dependent on interprovincial exports than the other regions. Such exports counts for 26.5 percent of shipments in Quebec, compared to 13 percent in British Columbia and 17 to 18 percent in the other provinces. On the other hand, Quebec is less dependent than other provinces on international markets for its exports of manufactured goods. International exports account for 35.6 percent of shipments for British Columbia, 31.3 percent for Ontario, and only 21.2 percent for Quebec.

Raynauld highlights the relative positions of the regions with respect to interregional trade with the following observations:

In percentage of shipments of region of origin

1.	Atlantic provinces to Quebec	8.8 percent
	Quebec to the Atlantic provinces	4.4 percent
2.	Ontario to Quebec	8.0 percent
	Quebec to Ontario	17.0 percent
3.	Prairie provinces to Quebec	3.8 percent
	Quebec to the Prairie provinces	3.3 percent

4. British Columbia to Quebec   1.7 percent
    Quebec to British Columbia   1.8 percent
5. Other provinces to Quebec   6.8 percent
    Quebec to the other provinces   26.5 percent

As Raynauld notes, Quebec is more than four times as dependent on the other provinces as other provinces are on Quebec and almost twice as dependent on Ontario as Ontario is on it. Nevertheless, Quebec and Ontario remain each other's most important markets. On the other hand, the Atlantic provinces are more dependent on Quebec. Bilateral trade with more distant provinces is less important.

TABLE 5

DESTINATION OF MANUFACTURING SHIPMENTS BY PROVINCE OR REGION OF ORIGIN, 1984
(Percent of Shipments)

Provinces of Origin				*Provinces of Destination*				
	Atlantic	Quebec	Ontario	Prairies	B.C.	Other Provinces	Outside Canada	Total
Atlantic	54.2	8.8	6.8	1.5	0.7	17.7	28.1	100.0
Quebec	4.4	52.3	17.0	3.3	1.8	26.5	21.2	100.0
Ontario	2.1	8.0	51.6	5.1	2.0	17.1	31.3	100.0
Prairies	0.8	3.8	7.3	69.4	6.0	17.7	12.9	100.0
British Columbia	0.3	1.7	3.3	8.3	51.1	13.8	35.4	100.0

Note: Total = Province of destination + Other provinces + Outside Canada
Source: Statistics Canada, *Destination of Shipments of Manufacturers 1984*, Catalogue 31-530 as cited in ASDEQ (1990, p.13).

Raynauld also presents data on the surplus or deficits on interprovincial trade which are shown in table 6. Ontario and Quebec are the two regions which have experienced large trade surpluses in manufacturing. In 1984 Ontario had a surplus of $8 billion; and Quebec, $3 billion. All other regions have registered deficits.

Raynauld also examined data on trade balances in energy, agriculture and minerals. Quebec had a deficit of $2.3 billion on energy trade in 1987, $523 million on agriculture in 1984, and $2.7 billion in non-

TABLE 6

SURPLUS OR DEFICIT IN INTERPROVINCIAL TRADE IN MANUFACTURED GOODS
(Millions of Dollars)

Provinces	Exports	Trade Imports	Surplus
Atlantic			
1967	259	1,129	-870
1974	727	2,210	-1,483
1979	1,519	3,664	-2,145
1984	1,805	5,206	-3,401
Quebec			
1967	3,289	3,005	284
1974	6,666	5,573	1,093
1979	10,524	9,807	717
1984	15,075	11,744	3,331
Ontario			
1967	5,548	2,591	2,957
1974	9,552	5,330	4,222
1979	17,620	8,781	8,839
1984	20,908	12,694	8,214
Prairies			
1967	684	2,252	-1,568
1974	1,600	4,007	-2,407
1979	3,090	8,160	-5,070
1984	4,071	9,687	-5,616
B.C.			
1967	470	1,273	-803
1974	1,002	2,427	-1,425
1979	1,986	4,326	-2,340
1984	2,486	5,015	-2,529
Canada			
1967	10,250	10,250	0
1974	19,547	19,547	0
1979	34,739	34,739	0
1984	44,347	44,347	0

Note: British Columbia includes the Yukon and Northwest Territories.

Source: Statistics Canada, Catalogue 31-504, 31-522, 31-530 as cited in Raynauld (1990, p.56).

transformed minerals. These figures suggest that Quebec is an advanced economy which exports manufactured products and imports raw materials. Raynauld argues that any measures to restrain this trade will have direct repercussions on Quebec's production, employment and income.

Raynauld makes a case that the integration of Quebec into the Canadian economy has enabled Quebec to grow more rapidly than Ontario and Canada in recent years. The gap in GDP per capita between Quebec and Ontario has narrowed from 25 percent in 1961 to 18 percent on average from 1986 to 1988. This progress could be threatened, he argues, if the integration between the Quebec and Canadian economies were disrupted as a result of Quebec's separation and the break-up of the Canadian common market.

Studies by major financial institutions

The Parti Québécois has often cited three studies done by major financial institutions as evidence of the economic viability of a sovereign Quebec (1990,pp.26-28). Another more recent study by a U.S. investment bank has also been the subject of some controversy.

Toronto Dominion Bank

The first study was done by the Toronto Dominion Bank (1990). In its policy paper arguing that sovereignty would have no impact on the Quebec economy, the Parti Québécois cites the Toronto Dominion Bank's study incorrectly:

> In a confidential study reported in the newspapers in March 1990, the Toronto-Dominion Bank (U.S. Division) concluded that regardless of the resolution of the constitutional issue, there will not be any economic uncertainty that will be harmful to Quebec in the short or long term (PQ, 1990, p.26, my translation).

But the study itself, which was written during the debate over the Meech Lake accord, does not say that sovereignty will have no harmful economic impact. Instead, the study says that "in the near term and long term...it is very unlikely that discussion about the Accord will have any effect on business confidence" (1990, p.2). The bank's study concluded only that discussions about the accord will not have any effect on business confidence; but the Parti Québécois incorrectly inferred that there would not be any effect from constitutional changes, including accession to sovereignty. This misinterpretation is an attempt by the Parti Québécois to gain greater credibility for its own views by putting them in the mouth of a respected financial institution.

In fact, the Toronto Dominion Bank study has nothing to say on the economic viability of a sovereign Québec. It does, however, provide a useful discussion of Canadian constitutional developments and the Meech Lake accord for its intended audience of American readers.

Merrill Lynch

Concerning the critical issue of the likely credit rating of a sovereign Quebec, the Parti Québécois cites Merrill Lynch as saying, "Given the economic strengths of the Province, one can argue that a 'sovereign' rating on Quebec would not be much different than its rating as a province" (1990, p.27). The Parti Québécois cites its source accurately, but it does not state that its source is a one-page comment prepared by an analyst, not a more detailed study of the financial viability of an independent Quebec.

The entire text on the Quebec economy takes just one paragraph, following three paragraphs of comments on the political implications of a failed Meech Lake accord:

> *If separate, how sound economically?* The gross domestic product of Quebec in 1988 was U.S. $120 billion. If it were an independent country, its GDP would exceed that of Denmark [$101 billion] and Austria [$117 billion] and fall slightly short of that of Belgium [$138 billion]. Since English language-only speakers represent a tiny 6.7 per cent of the total Quebec population, it is difficult to argue that there would be a damaging exodus of the English community. Many of the dissatisfied English have already departed for Ontario, having done so during the raucous 1970s. Québec's 6.5 million inhabitants represent about 25 % of Canada's population. The policies of the Bourassa government have been favourable to development. The economic growth over the last four years has been relatively balanced, adding diversification to the economy. Finally, the economic arguments advanced in the early 1980s suggested that the economic benefits are in close parity with the federal taxes paid. *Given the*

> *economic strengths of the Province, one can argue that a sovereign*
> *rating on Québec would not be much different than its rating as a*
> *province* . (Taylor, 1990)

Note that the fiscal balance studies discussed above do not, as claimed in the comment, suggest that the economic benefits to Québec are in close parity with federal taxes paid. Also Merrill Lynch says that the policies of the Bourassa government have been favourable to development. It does not say anything about how a Parti Québécois government is likely to be perceived by the financial community. It is also worth noting that Merrill Lynch is the lead underwriter for Quebec Hydro and that its interest in selling hydro bonds could cloud its objectivity in evaluating the likely international credit rating of a sovereign Quebec.

Bank of Montreal

A paper prepared by a Bank of Montreal employee (Close, 1989) has also been cited by the Parti Québécois to lend credibility to the view that Quebec sovereignty would not undermine investment (PQ, 1990, p.26). This study, which was prepared by a political scientist and for which neither the Bank of Montreal's Economics Department nor the bank takes any responsibility, provides an interesting discussion of the political forces shaping the North American economy in general and Quebec in particular. The section dealing with Quebec, which accounts for less than a quarter of the paper, focuses on the development of the new class of Quebec entrepreneurs and Quebec's economic development policies. It does not contain any economic analysis of the viability of a sovereign Quebec.

The passage which has attracted the most attention from sovereigntists is the following:

> Confederation or a separate state, however, is not the critical issue from an investment point of view. This is because Quebeckers are unlikely to vote for a separate state if it would endanger their standard of living; nor would the increasingly nationalistic business class lead Quebec out of Confederation if it would damage the newly emergent vibrant Quebec economy. The non-event of Norway's separation from Sweden in 1905 is perhaps the appropriate historic analogy for any legal separation of Quebec from the rest of Canada. (Close, 1989, p.4)

This passage says that Quebeckers are unlikely to separate if separation would damage the Quebec economy or reduce living standards. Thus, confederation versus separatism is not the key issue from an investment point of view. This is a political judgement about what Quebeckers are likely to do—not an economic one about the consequences of sovereignty. It says nothing about the implications for investment if sovereignty becomes economically damaging and if Quebeckers decide to ignore their economic self-interest and separate for reasons of national pride.

First Boston Corporation

In February a draft study done by First Boston Corporation (1991) on constitutional change in Canada was leaked to the press. This study created some controversy because it included a specific estimate of the risk premium in Quebec bonds and some erroneous estimates of the debt stock. The study was quickly revised and released without the offending estimate of the risk premium and debt stock error. The revised study now only reviews the constitutional debate, including Meech Lake, and the Allaire report, and it lays out the timetable for constitutional discussions. The study still warns that "the ongoing uncertainty probably means a higher premium on Canadian over US long term bonds will prevail for political reasons alone, regardless of economic fundamentals." The key passage in the study reads thus:

> As the new phase in the Constitutional debate begins, it introduces new uncertainties, For at least two years to come, a ferment of proposals, rhetoric and divisiveness will continue. What will result is unpredictable at this point, which creates an element of risk for investors. The impact could be greatest on foreign investors who do not have the full information necessary to interpret a complex legal, social and economic process, and who could react with an excess of caution to headline developments.

> A key index of the expense to Canada of the ongoing debate is in the spread of Canadian over US long-term bond yields. Of the 200-250 basis point spread that has prevailed for the last year, a portion probably reflects the uncertainty created by the Meech Lake debate. Other factors matter, too. In particular, relatively high Canadian short term rates of interest have driven up the

value of the Canadian dollar, and created the risk of depreciation sometime in the future. (1991, p.1)

A Quebec currency

While some economists have suggested that Canada might benefit from two or more currencies to combat regional disparities (Mundell, 1961, pp.657-65 and Dudley, 1973, pp.7-18), the consensus has been that the costs of an independent currency in terms of volatility and transaction costs would outweigh the advantages for an economy as small as Quebec's. In a study prepared for the Quebec government in 1979, Bernard Fortin argues that "the *smaller* an economy, the more *open* (in terms of trade and financial links with its partners in the monetary union), and the *less diversified* in its domestic production, the more it will benefit from a monetary union" (B. Fortin, 1979, p.10, as translated in Maxwell and Pestieau, 1980, p.37). This study provided the analytical underpinnings to support the Parti Québécois's preference for a monetary union.

More recently, a paper by David Laidler (1990), "Money after Meech," has had a big impact on the debate in Quebec about possible post-sovereignty currency arrangements. It has provided support from one of Canada's leading monetary economists for the proposition that a separate Quebec currency pegged to the U.S. dollar would be a viable second-best option for Quebec. Laidler argues that the prospect of a breakup of the Canadian monetary system would disturb international capital markets. Since Quebec has a strong interest in maintaining the current monetary system and other economic ties, he argues, Quebec may need to retain a federal government in which it is represented. Laidler sees threats to the Canadian monetary system from several directions. Western populism could endanger the cohesiveness of the Canadian monetary union. The inability of the Bank of Canada to retain its price stability goal in the face of political opposition could make it unattractive for Quebec to continue to participate in the Canadian monetary system. Or the rest of Canada could try to exact too high a price from Quebec for a maintenance of monetary ties. In this case, in Laidler's view, the best option for Quebec would be to establish a separate currency pegged to the U.S. dollar.

Laidler emphasizes the attachment of a responsible Quebec government to price stability and a hard currency. His paper was written before the Quebec business community's dissatisfaction with the Bank of Canada's current monetary policy became apparent in their submissions to the Bélanger-Campeau Commission (see *inter alia* the Chamber of Commerce submission). In fact, arguments have been made before the Bélanger-Campeau Commission for sovereignty—or at least Quebec's input into the conduct of monetary policy—in order to get lower interest rates and a cheaper Canadian dollar, which would improve the competitive position of Quebec industry. Quebec's attachment to a hard currency is probably weaker than Laidler suggests.

Laidler's paper contains a very good discussion of what is important for a currency. He argues that foreign creditors and investors do not really care about Canadian constitutional discord as long as it neither threatens to generate economic instability nor affects confidence in Canada's capacity and willingness to service its present debts. But the prospect that Quebec might introduce a separate currency unnerves international capital markets: it raises questions about the redenomination of Canadian dollar debt and the possible impact on the profitability of investment of market inefficiencies resulting from the breakup of the Canadian monetary union.

For the establishment of a Quebec dollar to have more than a symbolic meaning, Laidler argues, its value would have to be potentially variable against the Canadian dollar. Countries which have GDPs of the same order of magnitude as Quebec, such as Finland, Denmark, Norway, and Austria, all have their own currencies, but none of them are freely floating. To him, this suggests that Quebec might not choose a flexible exchange rate regime.

If a currency already exists, Laidler argues, a floating rate may be preferable to a pegged. But the nuisance costs of having a separate currency and establishing its viability may be too large to justify creating it in the first place. The nuisance costs of maintaining a separate currency increase as the economy becomes more open and its size decrease, while the benefits from a separate flexible rate currency decrease as the economy's openness increases and its size decreases.

Laidler describes how the adjustment mechanism works with fixed and floating exchange rates and how a flexible exchange rate is a better adjustment tool when an economy is larger and less open. Laidler correctly dismisses the argument that it is possible to use monetary independence and a floating Quebec dollar to promote low unemployment and rapid growth; in fact, all that monetary independence can determine in the long run is the rate of inflation. But he overestimates the attractiveness of the Bank of Canada's strong and credible anti-inflation credentials to a more independent Quebec government.

Highlighted by Laidler are the problems involved in establishing a new currency for Quebec. People must be persuaded to use it. Its use can be encouraged inside Quebec through government decrees, such as requiring taxes to be paid in Quebec dollars or enforcing only contracts denominated in Quebec dollars. Gaining acceptance internationally for a Quebec currency would be more difficult because of the need to overcome concerns that the new government would follow inflationary policies. According to Laidler, Quebec could try to borrow viability for its new dollar by establishing a fixed exchange rate; this strategy would be more likely to succeed if the U.S. dollar were used as the reference rate. If the Canadian dollar were chosen, there would be more suspicion that the Quebec government would pursue inflationary policies and its currency would devalue.

Nevertheless, Laidler makes a very strong case for the continuation of the existing Canadian monetary union. He believes that Quebec will accept the case. First, the maintenance of the current Canadian financial system with widespread branching, which does much to promote capital mobility and to give the system stability, requires the continued existence of some system-wide and politically responsible regulatory authority. Second, the maintenance of a common currency would keep the burden of adjustment to shocks to the Quebec economy from elsewhere in Canada focused on the local labour market. A common labour market is a useful supplement to a currency union which goes together with a common market for goods and services, but it requires a common political authority. Laidler accepts that this political authority might be a radically redesigned and less centralized government—a Confederation, of which Quebec would be a member. He argues that the maintenance of a common Canadian currency for a common Canadian labour and goods market would make it possible to negotiate other aspects of Confederation without the threat of a foreign exchange crisis.

Financing government deficits and debt

The division of the federal government debt is an important issue which would have to be addressed in any negotiations over sovereignty. Though there has not been any rigorous analysis of the economic impact of this issue, some interesting views have been expressed and the issue is so important that it cannot be ignored.

First, Grant Reuber (1990, p.B4) argued that Quebec would have a substantial bargaining advantage in resolving this issue since Canada's public debt is an obligation of the government of Canada. Given this substantial bargaining advantage for Quebec, separation would almost certainly result in the rest of Canada being left with a disproportionate share of today's federal debt compared with the revenue base remaining to service it. Douglas Purvis (1990) responded by calling the federal government debt "the bonds that tie" and by suggesting that it adds a greater degree of mutual interest than was present a decade ago. In his view, there are two reasons for this. First, Quebec will continue to be dependent on foreign capital and cannot afford to welch on its current obligations; second, Quebec will need to preserve strong economic ties with the rest of Canada.

More recently, Jacques Parizeau has reassured English Canadians that even a Parti Québécois government would not seek to avoid its share of the debt. In a speech to the Empire and Canadian Clubs in Toronto, he said the following:

> What share? There are really two criteria to use: population and gross domestic product. We will, I suppose, haggle for a few weeks before we come to something like a quarter. (Parizeau, 1990, pp.9-10)

Marcel Côté has argued in a pair of interesting papers (1990a,b) that Quebec could not assume its $100 billion or so share of the federal debt overnight. He notes that the national debt is not a passive debt—half of it is short-term and the other half has a maturity of only seven years. While he thinks that the Quebec government can in theory support such a level of debt, it will take five to ten years to develop a market for $100 billion of Quebec debt. So, he argues, the old debt will remain a common debt, with Quebec obliged to send regular debt servicing payments to Ottawa. Jacques Parizeau shares this view (1990, p.9-10). Nevertheless,

Côté argues that there would be a $1 billion or so risk premium per year associated with financing the cost of the debt.

Côté also raises some question about the ability of the Quebec government to finance its share of the federal deficit. If the Quebec government deficit were to increase from $2 billion to $10 billion (4 to 5 percent of Quebec GDP), there would be no market for such a huge annual increase in the level of debt and it would take years to develop one.

Another important aspect of the deficit and debt has arisen in the debate on Quebec sovereignty. The disequilibrium in the federal budget has been one of the Quebec business communities' main sources of dissatisfaction and frustration with Canadian federalism (Chambre de Commerce du Québec, 1990, p.11). Rightly or wrongly, it affirms the idea among businesspeople that Canadian federalism has been an economic failure and that a sovereign Quebec could perhaps do better.

Uncertainty

The Association des Economistes Québécois brief to the Bélanger-Campeau Commission emphasizes that the process on which Quebec and Canada are now embarked involves much uncertainty and certain important economic risks (1990, p.20). Since the consequences of this process on economic activity in Quebec and Canada depend enormously on the political dynamic and political currents, the brief cautions decision-makers to act with prudence. While no quantitative estimates are provided of the likely impact on the economy, two illustrative scenarios are sketched out to show the importance of the process. In the first scenario, the transmission of powers takes place in serenity; in the second, it takes place in an atmosphere of rancour and discord. In the first, the Quebec and Canadian government work together to reduce the deficit by eliminating duplication. There is a smooth transition to new monetary arrangements. Interest rates come down. The climate for investment improves. In the second, there is fighting over all aspects of the transfer of powers, including the new monetary regime. Investors become upset, triggering an exchange crisis. Interest rates have to be raised to support the two new currencies, probably after devaluations. The climate of uncertainty has a negative impact on the investment and economic activity.

While no quantitative information is available on the impact of uncertainty in the current situation, André Raynauld (1990, pp. 45-47) provides some data on the movement of head offices out of and into Quebec and on immigration during the 1980 referendum period. Based on an earlier study, he reports the following movements of head offices:

	Out	In	Balance
1979	282	79	-203
1980	183	68	-115
1981	164	91	-73
Total	629	238	-391

Raynauld observes that, while political uncertainty was not the only factor behind the movement of head offices out of Quebec, it is significant that the outflow decreased and the inflow increased after the referendum.

Raynauld presents the following figures on net immigration from Quebec:

1966-71	-10,566
1971-76	-3,323
1976-81	-17,063
1981-86	-2,573
1986-89	+18,723

The data show, according to Raynauld, that immigration flows are extremely sensitive to political developments. He cites the fivefold increase in net outmigration from 1976 to 1981 following the election of the Parti Québécois and the 1980 referendum, and, afterwards, the dramatic decline in net outmigration and ultimate reversal.

In its brief to the Bélanger-Campeau Commission, the Quebec Chamber of Commerce also provides some interesting data on investment trends during the 1980 referendum period. Investment per capita in Quebec fell from 102 percent of that in Ontario in 1979 to only 90 percent in 1981, before rebounding to 97 percent in 1984. The Chamber notes that, while there were several factors that contributed to the fall in investment, it would be difficult to argue that political uncertainty surrounding the 1980 referendum had nothing to do with the fall (1990, p.7).

Conclusion

The only strong conclusion that can be drawn from the survey of the pre-Bélanger-Campeau literature presented in this chapter is that there is still a scarcity of up-to-date hard analysis on the costs and benefits of Confederation and on the economic impact of Quebec sovereignty. Most of the serious studies were done in the late 1970s when the election of a Parti Québécois government and the prospects of a referendum on sovereignty-association focused attention on the issue. These were the studies done by the Canadian Unity Information Office and the C.D. Howe Institute's Accent Quebec Program. The empirical information and many of the conclusions contained in these studies are now largely out-of-date. The more recent studies have been completed quickly and are not as rigorous. Good economic studies of all aspects of the economic consequences of Quebec sovereignty are desperately needed so that important decisions about the future of the country will not have to be made without an adequate understanding of the facts. As we will see in the next chapter, the Bélanger-Campeau economic studies provide some useful additional information, albeit from a largely sovereigntist perspective, but the need for further objective analysis still remains urgent.

Chapter 3

The Bélanger-Campeau's Sovereigntist Economic Studies

Introduction

THIS CHAPTER PROVIDES A CRITIQUE and summary of the background economic studies prepared for the Bélanger-Campeau Commission by outside experts, the secretariat of the commission, and the Ministry of Finance (Commission sur l'avenir politique et constitutionnel du Québec, 1991b). The authors of the studies include some of Quebec's most distinguished economists. The nine studies considered deal with trade relations, public finances, labour markets, macroeconomic policy coordination, and monetary options.

It is important to consider these studies in detail because of their key role in shaping the opinion of the Quebec elite on the economic consequences of sovereignty. Because the studies have not been translated into English and have only been published in limited quantities, they have not received wide dissemination outside of Quebec, even among economists. English Canadians need to be familiar with the main arguments made in these studies if they are to be informed participants in the national debate on the economic consequences of Quebec sovereignty.

The studies done by the individual economists contain much useful analysis and are generally well done, albeit from a largely sovereigntist perspective. The Secretariat drew on the other studies to produce a more political, less analytical and even more sovereigntist paper than those of the individual economists.

All the studies share two assumptions: transitional costs of Quebec sovereignty will be minimal if economic rationality prevails in the establishment of economic relations with the rest of Canada, and the long-run costs of Quebec sovereignty are negligible. Nothing in these studies supports these assumptions. A thorough assessment of these studies is thus in order.

The studies take a consistently optimistic approach. In chapters on trade relations, for example, it is taken as a matter of course that trade relations between Quebec and the rest of Canada and the United States would be unaffected by separation. Canada is expected to be willing to agree to a common market with Quebec. The United States is portrayed as ready to conclude a free trade agreement with Quebec immediately. The studies do not mention the possibility that hard feelings engendered by the separation could make reestablishment of trade between Quebec and Canada difficult. Nor do they mention that trade negotiations are time consuming and that the United States may have other priorities than negotiating a free trade agreement with Quebec and that when it did it would most likely want to negotiate changes that would be disadvantageous for Quebec. The costs of negotiations with both Canada and the United States are completely ignored. The importance of harmonization of policies with Canada to preserve a common market is stressed, but there is no appreciation of how difficult this would be for two separate states.

Another example of optimism is the view that Quebec could unilaterally decide to establish a monetary union with Canada by declaring the Canadian dollar legal tender and by establishing clearing arrangements with members of the Canadian Payments Association. The possibility that such a monetary union may not be desired by Canada and that Canada could block it by refusing to supply currency and clearing arrangements is not even considered. Aside from this central optimistic assumption adopted by the secretariat in its papers, the study by Bernard Fortin on the monetary options contained a very good discussion of the advantages of monetary union.

A final example of optimism bordering on outright deception is the analysis of the financial position of a sovereign Quebec. The secretariat of the commission estimates that, before taking into account the division of assets and liabilities, the budgetary position of a sovereign Quebec would be basically unaffected (using 1990-91 as the reference year). This result is difficult to reconcile with the secretariat's own estimate in study 7 that Quebec's net fiscal gain would be $2.7 billion in 1988.

The secretariat also proposes that Quebec should only assume 18.5 percent of the public debt based on its share of assets (defined in an unconventional way to include the cumulated deficit) instead of its 25.4 percent population share. The secretariat argues based on the opinions of two experts in international law that this is compatible with international law. A closer reading of the legal opinions reveals that almost any share agreed to by the two parties would be compatible with international law. The secretariat's proposal thus has no special legal status even though the secretariat certainly seeks to create the impression that it does.

While the increased debt under the secretariat's proposal would raise Quebec's budgetary deficit to $9,282 or 5.8 percent of GDP and would increase Quebec's debt burden as a share of GDP from 26.4 percent to 63.9 percent, it would leave the Quebec debt to GDP ratio well below the 72.1 percent ratio of Canada. It would also be comparable to the level of European countries. In effect, the secretariat chose a share of the debt much lower than Quebec's share of population to enable it to present an artificially rosy financial position for a sovereign Quebec.

Important exceptions to the optimistic approach are the papers on trade by Pierre-Paul Proulx and Guilain Cauchy, those on labour markets by Pierre Fortin, and those on international financial integration by Daniel Racette.

The secretariat's historical analysis of the fiscal benefits Quebec derived from Confederation ignores the massive transfers from the Prairies to the rest of Canada as a result of regulated oil prices. The study therefore substantially understates Quebec's fiscal benefits from Confederation from 1973 to 1985. For recent years, the estimates of benefits are more reasonable, with Quebec enjoying a fiscal benefit of $409 per capita in 1988.

In my critique, I examine the nine studies separately.

Study 1

"The Maintenance of Access to External Markets: Some Judicial Questions Raised under the Hypothesis of Quebec Sovereignty," by Ivan Bernier

(Commission, 1991b, pp.1-17)

This study provides the opinion of Ivan Bernier, a noted Quebec international legal specialist, on several questions on Quebec's right of access to international and Canadian markets under the existing trade treaties if Quebec were to become sovereign. The treaties considered are the General Agreements on Tariffs and Trade (GATT), of which Canada is a member, and the Canada-U.S. Free Trade Agreement. His opinion is based on solid legal grounds, as one would expect from so eminent an international legal authority. He only enters on shaky ground when he speculates about the likely results of the political process.

According to Bernier, under GATT there are two ways for a newly independent state to become a member: 1) accession by means of negotiations under article XXXIII, and 2) accession by means of succession under article XXVI. The problem with negotiations is that they are often lengthy and require the approval of two-thirds of the members. Succession was established to accommodate newly independent countries resulting from decolonialization. To qualify under succession, Quebec would have to accept Canada's engagements for the territory of Quebec and would in turn be recognized as a member of GATT retroactively from the date of independence.

Bernier also addresses the question of what membership in GATT would do to ensure continued access to Canadian markets. Under GATT Canada could apply to Quebec the existing tariffs applied to GATT members, unless of course Quebec were to conclude a customs union or free trade agreement with Canada. GATT would prevent Canada from placing quantitative restrictions on imports from Quebec. Exception to this would be restrictions related to classification or quality control and agricultural products. This would include agricultural products under supply management. GATT protection would also not apply to government purchases and internal subsidies to national production, unless Quebec were to sign the three codes dealing with these problems that came from the Tokyo round. In the case of subsidies, Quebec could respond to Canadian subsidies by using its compensating rights under article VI.

Bernier speculates on which international regulations would apply if Quebec were to try to use the right of succession to gain membership in the Canada-U.S. Free Trade Agreement. He notes that before the 1978 Vienna Convention the principle was *tabula rasa*, that is, treaties binding the predecessor state did not bind the successor state. Afterwards, as a result of pressure from Third World states, the suggested principle was one of continuity of the full rights of the treaty for the successor state. Nevertheless, Bernier argues Quebec should not expect to gain full accession to the free trade treaty because neither the rule prior to the Vienna convention nor the new rule would apply to the successor state, Quebec. Bernier convincingly asserts that a trilateral treaty would be radically different than a bilateral treaty. He neglects to mention that neither Canada nor the United States have yet signed the Vienna convention. Bernier argues that the agreement would become applicable to Quebec by right of succession after agreement was reached with Canada and the United States on the necessary changes. In the interim, the agreement would become de facto applicable. However, in doing so he goes beyond the grounds of a legal opinion and into the realm of political speculation.

The final question that Bernier considers is how would the Americans react to a Quebec request to join the Canada-U.S. Free Trade Agreement. This is obviously an exercise in pure political speculation. The position he adopts is extremely optimistic. He argues that it is improbable that Canada and the United States would try to take advantage of Quebec's accession to sovereignty to exclude Quebec from the agreement, to impose more burdensome conditions on Quebec, or to demand that Canada and Quebec renegotiate the agreement. He trustingly believes that the United States would favour a solution that would impede the development of instability and conflict in Canada. He claims that the simplest solution would be to extend to Quebec the application of the existing agreement as is.

Bernier notes that the U.S. could try to resolve the contentious issues of trade in alcoholic beverages or agricultural supply management, but he believes that this would not be very probable because it would be difficult to impose a new regime in these areas without doing the same to the rest of Canada. What Bernier overlooks is that these areas would be under the jurisdiction of a sovereign Quebec, but not under the jurisdiction of the Canadian federal government. The U.S. appreciates the difficulty of the Canadian federal government has in committing the provinces, so they made allowances for this in the free trade negotiations. In negotiating with a sovereign Quebec, there would be no need to make such allowances.

Bernier claims it would be curious for the U.S. not to negotiate with Quebec given its readiness to negotiate an agreement with the Mexicans. This is perhaps true, but Bernier should not underestimate the relative importance of Mexico and Quebec in U.S. eyes. Mexico is a country with over 85 million people. The U.S. knows that it either has to conclude an agreement or be faced with an even greater inflow of illegal immigration from Mexico. The potential for political instability is also many times greater in Mexico than in Quebec.

Bernier's assessment of the likely U.S. reaction to a Quebec request for membership in the Canada-U.S. Free Trade Agreement is naive. Although he is correct that the U.S. would eventually want to have a free trade agreement with Quebec, a number of issues would have to be resolved before concluding an agreement. The greater degree of government intervention in the economy in Quebec would attract the critical attention of U.S. negotiators. Furthermore, a free trade agreement with Quebec may not be the U.S. government's highest priority. The administration could not conclude an agreement with Quebec without a negotiating mandate from Congress. The current trade bill gives the administration the authorization to negotiate fast track agreements with Canada, Mexico, and GATT; it could be used for a similar agreement with Quebec. But Congress extracted a commitment from the administration that it would be consulted about the specifics of the agreement—presumably about any agreement with Quebec as well. Once an agreement is reached and if Congressional concerns are not taken into account, the Administration could have trouble getting the final agreement approved by Congress. The bottom line is that the whole process could take a long time and in the interval Quebec industry could find itself deprived of access to the U.S. market under the free trade agreement. Bernier's discussion shows no appreciation of the realities of the U.S. political and legislative process.

Study 2

"The Access of Quebec to External Markets and the Canadian Economic Space," by the Secretariat

(Commission, 1991b, pp.19-54)

This study, which was prepared by the secretariat of the Bélanger-Campeau Commission and draws on the legal opinion that Bernier gives in his study, focuses on the implications of Quebec sovereignty for its external economic relations with Canada, the United States and the rest of the world.

According to the secretariat's study the Quebec economy is very open, with 33 percent of its production and 48 percent of its manufacturers' shipments going outside the province. Exports of goods and services are divided with 60 percent going to the rest of Canada and 40 percent to other countries. The United States accounts for 80 percent of Quebec exports outside of Canada. The dependence of the Quebec economy on markets in other provinces at 20 percent of production is higher than the average of the other provinces. This degree of dependence remained constant from 1974 to 1984. No comparisons are made with the rest of Canada as a whole. It is these comparisons that are most relevant from a point of view of the relative degree of external dependence of a sovereign Quebec. The secretariat also notes that the importance of markets outside of Canada has grown under the auspices of GATT and that this is likely to continue under the free trade agreement, but that the rest of Canada will always be a major market for Quebec production.

The judicial and institutional framework for Quebec foreign trade

The secretariat's study discusses GATT, which regulates Quebec's access to international markets, in some detail, emphasizing the reduction in tariffs on industrial products from an average of 40 percent in 1947 to 5 percent in 1987 and the liberalization of trading rules. The secretariat itemizes the gaps in GATT coverage: partial rather than full access to public sector markets, quantitative restrictions in certain sectors, and the exclusion of services. The secretariat's overall conclusion is that GATT guarantees substantial access to the markets of other countries to all signatories independent of their size. Furthermore, if a compromise could be reached on agriculture, the Uruguay round would probably be concluded, which would significantly liberalize trade in services, public sector markets, textiles, and agricultural products.

The secretariat summarizes the main aspects of the Canada-U.S. Free Trade Agreement and emphasizes the respects in which it goes beyond GATT. The secretariat notes that the free trade agreement will increase the degree of integration of Quebec with the United States, but that, even when the FTA is fully implemented in 1999, the degree of integration will be less than with the rest of Canada.

The Canadian economic space

The secretariat stresses the importance of maintaining the existing Canadian economic space with its almost complete free flow of people, goods, services, and capital, which constitutes a real common market. The Charter right of all Canadian citizens to establish themselves and earn their living in any province is mentioned. The extent to which this is qualified by rules concerning accreditation and the exercise of trades and professions is noted, as is the importance of the transferability of social programs such as unemployment insurance, medical care, and pensions in facilitating mobility.

Section 121 of the Constitution Act of 1867 is cited as guaranteeing the free circulation of goods within Canada. In combination with the federal government's power over commercial policy and customs, the Canadian provinces were able to form a customs union to avoid the need to control goods at provincial borders. On the other hand, the secretariat notes that provinces have interfered with the free flow of goods through product standards, public sector purchasing policy, and other measures. Provincial efforts at harmonization and agreements have helped to reduce the restrictive effects of these measures, but they remain limited. Examples of provincial restrictions cited are preferential policies of provincial liquor control boards, the requirements of local production of beer, and supply management marketing boards for milk, poultry, and eggs.

The free flow of services is not guaranteed by section 121, but by the general freedom to do business anywhere in Canada. The secretariat attributes the free flow of capital to the exclusive responsibility of the federal government for money, banking and the rate of interest. The existence of a common currency and a national system of banking are regarded as being of particular importance, as is the freedom of firms to invest anywhere in the country. The tax collection agreements are mentioned as another important element of harmonization. The Macdonald Commission proposal for a code of economic conduct to protect the Canadian common market to which the federal and provincial governments would adhere is discussed. But the Macdonald Commission did not recommend that such a code be enshrined in the Constitution because the Canadian economic union works well enough and the restrictions on interprovincial trade do not have a large enough impact on economic activity to justify an in-depth constitutional reform.

The maintenance of Quebec's foreign trade

The secretariat observes that the trade relations of a sovereign Quebec with countries other than Canada and the U.S. would be governed by GATT. This section of the study draws heavily on Bernier's opinion discussed above. Succession under article XXVI of the General Agreement is the preferred route to membership in GATT. If done, Quebec would have to adopt the Canadian tariff schedule at the time of separation and membership would be retroactive to the same date. The secretariat says that Quebec's participation in GATT would be conditioned by Quebec's arrangement with the rest of Canada. Quebec and Canada could adopt a common commercial policy and speak with one voice at GATT. In my view, however, this is not very likely given the difficulty of coming to a common agreement on commercial policy. The secretariat mentions the 25 restraint agreements for textile and clothing under the multi-fibre agreement which would have to be renegotiated, but neglects to mention the controversy which would arise between Canada and Quebec, with its extensive textile and clothing industry, over renegotiation. More generally, the secretariat does not seem to attach very much significance to the time and resources which must go into reaching trade agreements.

The secretariat emphasizes that the continued participation of Quebec in the Canada-U.S. Free Trade Agreement is essential to the maintenance and improvement of the competitive position of Quebec business. Again relying on Bernier's opinion that succession would not apply and that a third party joining a bilateral treaty would change radically the existing bilateral treaty, the secretariat argues that in theory a sovereign Quebec could be required to renegotiate and sign the free trade agreement with the U.S. But, it is argued, the agreement could become applicable to Quebec by right of succession if Canada and the United States were agreeable. And the U.S. would be likely to accept Quebec in the agreement without substantial modifications to avoid the development of instability and conflicts in Quebec. A refusal by the U.S. would interfere with the establishment of a common commercial policy between Canada and Quebec and would force Quebec to look for political and economic links elsewhere. It would also be against the American interest in guaranteed access to Quebec hydroelectricity. The secretariat supports Bernier's view that the U.S. would not take advantage of the situation to resolve outstanding issues such as trade in alcoholic beverages and agricultural supply management. But in my view, the difficulties of reaching an agreement quickly with the U.S. are significantly underestimated. The secretariat shows no appreciation of the way trade policy is made in the U.S. and the different roles of the administration and Congress. It also does not recognize the tough-minded mood on trade policy now prevalent in Congress as evidenced by the difficulties the administration had in getting the recent trade bill approved by Congress.

The secretariat candidly acknowledges that the degree of integration and harmonization between Quebec and the rest of Canada would be difficult to maintain because a sovereign Quebec could follow different policies than the rest of Canada. The maintenance of the common market would require that the national policies of Quebec and Canada continue to be harmonized in areas such as money, internal and external commercial policy, and legislation and regulations affecting the free flow of goods, services, persons and capital. As for mechanisms which would regulate policy coordination, the secretariat concentrates exclusively on those which would not require reassociation with Canada, thereby showing that it would still be possible to maintain the most important features of a common market without a formal agreement. The secretariat does argue though that such an agreement would be in the best interest of both partners. Also, the absence of a general agreement would not preclude sectoral agreements as the 170 existing bilateral treaties between Canada and the United States demonstrate. But the secretariat does not mention that these treaties have been negotiated and have evolved over more than one hundred years. It would be unrealistic to expect such a complicated web of treaties to emerge between Quebec and Canada except over a very long period of time. It takes much time and effort to negotiate and ratify a treaty.

The secretariat addresses the key issue of money based on the discussion contained in the paper by Bernard Fortin (study 6). The two questions considered are whether to adopt a Quebec currency and how to determine monetary policy if Quebec continues to use the Canadian dollar. The costs of establishing a Quebec currency which are cited are transaction costs and exchange risk. An estimate of the magnitude of these costs in the European Economic Community (ECC) of one percent of GDP, which is discussed more fully in study 6, is mentioned. The secretariat reports that the application of this figure to Canada gives a cost estimate of a separate Quebec currency of $1.6 billion in 1990. This is obviously a very rough and not particularly reliable estimate. The costs could easily be higher for an economy as small and as open as Quebec. The secretariat correctly observes that it would be difficult to maintain a true common market with Canada without a common currency. It also warns that a separate currency for Quebec would run counter to the global trend to fewer currencies or currency blocks and fixed exchange rates.

The secretariat juxtaposes the gains of a common money with the loss of monetary autonomy. It also acknowledges that a Quebec currency that was tied to the Canadian or U.S. dollar would not give much autonomy to Quebec monetary policy. A sovereign Quebec would have to establish confidence in the Quebec currency and could not pursue a more expansionary policy without being subject to sanctions from international markets.

To conserve the monetary elements of the existing common market, the secretariat argues a jointly determined monetary policy is not necessary and the only condition that must be met is the use of a common money. This could be done through the establishment of legislation that would retain the Canadian dollar as legal tender in Quebec. Quebec financial institutions could make arrangements for banknotes and change through the Canadian payments association. According to the secretariat, nothing could stop Quebec from conducting its transactions in Canadian dollars. But, although the Canadian government could nt stop Quebec from using Canadian dollars, it could certainly make it difficult by refusing to supply currency and to establish clearing arrangements. The proportion of Canadian currency circulating in Quebec would wear out over time and would have to be replaced. It would be virtually impossible to run a Canadian dollar-based monetary system in Quebec without access to Canadian currency on a continuing basis. The secretariat fails to anticipate these difficulties in its report. The secretariat notes that Quebec could seek to negotiate a say in the Bank of Canada decisions, but it is realistic in recognizing that such a say would not be great and would be of secondary importance. The secretariat raises the issue of Quebec's share of the seigneurage or profits of the Bank of Canada, which would also be tied up with the question of the division of assets and debt. The secretariat argues strongly that a monetary union would be the best option for both Canada and Quebec if Quebec were to separate. This is undoubtedly true, but the monetary union would be stronger and better if Quebec were to remain in Canada.

The secretariat argues that a customs union is also necessary for the preservation of the most complete free trade between Canada and Quebec. This could be done by ratifying an agreement that would reestablish the free trade currently sanctioned by article 121 of the Constitution Act of 1867 and by renouncing tariffs and quantitative restrictions allowed under GATT. If this were not done, $100 billion in trade would be affected, raising prices to consumers and reducing productivity. The establishment of customs controls between Quebec and Canada would in themselves impose important costs on travellers and business enterprises. A free trade agreement would not be sufficient to avoid such controls because of the need to verify the origins of goods to make sure they were produced within the free trade zone.

The secretariat recognizes that a free trade agreement would result in a divergence of commercial policies. It acknowledges that Canada might not wish to retain a protectionist regime for textiles, clothing and dairy production which are concentrated in Quebec. But it also notes that other provinces, including particularly Ontario, benefit from protection. In the case of industrial milk, the secretariat argues that, while Canada could modify the system of provincial quotas and import restraints, the negative effects for Quebec producers would be limited by the nature of the industry and by GATT. Under article XI of GATT, the secretariat argues, Canada could not put in place restrictions which would reduce the proportion of imports in domestic consumption to a level lower than before restrictions were in place. Canada could import more from less costly third country producers, but this would be damaging to the Canadian industry. I think that the application of article XI in the case of a breakup of a country is debatable. If Quebec were to separate, it would be in Canada's interest to allow domestic dairy producers to increase production in return for lower prices. It would be difficult to see GATT seriously impeding the process. The secretariat is realistic in observing that, in the context of the current GATT negotiations, the Canada-U.S. Free Trade Agreement and the trilateral negotiations with Mexico, protection will have to decrease in the future.

Concerning the free circulation of people, the secretariat makes the interesting observation that Quebec anglophones are 15 times more mobile than Quebec francophones and would benefit most from the preservation of mobility rights. The secretariat suggests that the way to preserve freedom of movement would be through new mechanisms which would maintain the right of establishment and work presently in the Canadian Charter of Rights and Freedoms. The secretariat also argues that a maintenance of labour mobility would require that rights to the main social programs such as unemployment insurance, medicare, and pensions continue to be transferable across boundaries. In my view, this would be highly unlikely.

The secretariat maintains that after becoming sovereign Quebec would have to maintain in force most of existing federal legislation and to respect subsequently the appropriate degree of harmonization. Specific important examples cited are the regulation of banks, competition policy, trademarks, copyrights, bankruptcy, and transportation regulations. Taxes including income taxes and the GST would have to continue to be harmonized. On a more technical level, it would be necessary to harmonize the post office, weights and measures, industrial property, and telecommunications. The secretariat, however, fails to acknowledge the great difficulty of harmonizing policy in all of these areas. Nor does it mention that if Quebec loses its voice in the determination of Canadian policy, a policy of harmonization would give a sovereign Quebec less say in all these important policy areas than it had as a province.

Study 3

"An Examination of Quebec Trade with the other Canadian Provinces, the United States, and the rest of the World," by Pierre-Paul Proulx and Guilain Cauchy

(Commission, 1991b, pp.55-165)

Proulx and Cauchy's study is a thorough and comprehensive examination of Quebec's trade relations with the rest of Canada, the United States, and the rest of the world. It builds on some of the earlier studies of Proulx. It is primarily descriptive and presents the most up-to-date data on Quebec trade flows including some previously unpublished data from the Statistics Canada and the Quebec Bureau of Statistics. Proulx and Cauchy make use of the neoclassical framework of international trade theory as embodied in the Hecksher-Ohlin theorem to shed some light on Quebec's trade flows. Proulx and Cauchy do not discuss the desirability of Quebec sovereignty.

Interprovincial trade

Proulx and Cauchy begin the study with a brief survey of the literature on Quebec's trade. They then quickly turn to a review of the most recent data on Quebec trade. For interprovincial trade, data from the Quebec Bureau of Statistics and Statistics Canada on the destination of manufacturers' shipments were used. Proulx and Cauchy note that in 1984 Quebec was the region most dependent on interprovincial shipments. The high but decreasing dependence of Quebec on Ontario is noted. The importance of the proximity of markets and transportation costs in determining Quebec's trade with the other Canadian regions is emphasized. The high degree of self supply that Quebec shares with Ontario is also noted. Proulx and Cauchy observe that Quebec and Ontario are the only two Canadian provinces that have a surplus in trade in manufactured goods. They cite the $3.3 billion surplus in 1984 and indicate the importance of clothing, metal fabrication, and paper and allied products. The large deficits in food and machinery are noted. The fact that Ontario is Quebec's most important domestic market—receiving 64 percent of Quebec interprovincial shipments in 1984—is highlighted.

International trade in the primary and secondary sectors

Primarily using data published by the Quebec Bureau of Statistics, Proulx and Cauchy explore Quebec's international trade in the primary and secondary sectors. According to them, Quebec was traditionally seen as an exporter of primary materials and as an importer of manufactured goods. But more recent data show that Quebec has performed well in exporting manufactured goods internationally compared to the rest of Canada and even to all other industrialized countries. While Quebec is somewhat less open than the rest of Canada, Quebec has a respectable position as an exporter, ranking seventeenth in importance near Switzerland, Sweden and Australia. The United States is Quebec's largest trading partner outside of Canada, receiving 77 percent of Quebec's exports in 1987. But Quebec does relatively little trade with the dynamic markets of Japan and South East Asia. Proulx and Cauchy argue that Quebec should seek to diversify its trade more in this direction.

Quebec's overall deficit in international trade is contrasted with Canada's overall surplus. Proulx and Cauchy make no mention of the difficulties that such a deficit might pose for a sovereign Quebec.

Proulx and Cauchy list the fifteen most important exports and imports of Quebec. On the export side, newsprint is the most important, but aluminium and alloys are catching up. On the import side, automobiles are in first place. The deficit in trade in automobiles was $1.4 billion in 1989. Proulx and Cauchy find this disturbing and characterize the automobile industry as the Achilles heel of Quebec's external trade. They overstate their point.

Quebec's position at the national and international level in 1984

Proulx and Cauchy use the 1984 data on trade from Statistic Canada's provincial input-output table to give a more precise estimate of Quebec's interprovincial and international trade flows. The data show that Quebec comes second—far behind Ontario—in trading volume, accounting for 25 percent of shipments to Canada and 17 percent of foreign exports. Quebec had a deficit in interprovincial trade of $1 billion in 1984 and a deficit of $3.2 billion internationally for a total deficit of $4.2 billion. Again Proulx and Cauchy do not comment upon the significance of such a deficit for a sovereign Quebec. The dominance of Ontario in service trade is noted. It is the only province to have a surplus. In contrast, Quebec is in balance on service trade. Quebec's 1984 surplus of $1.1 billion in textiles and clothing is noted. Proulx and Cauchy comment that it is regrettable that more recent data are not available to assess the impact of the Canada-U.S. Free Trade Agreement.

International and interprovincial trade of different sectors of production for Quebec and other provinces in 1974, 1979, and 1984

Proulx and Cauchy use data compiled by the Economic Council of Canada on interprovincial trade including primary, secondary, and tertiary trade to compare the performance of Quebec exports in Canadian and international markets. Quebec's share in interprovincial exports has decreased from 28.2 percent in 1974 to 23.5 percent in 1984—the only region in which interprovincial exports decreased during this period. In contrast, Quebec's share of foreign exports increased from 17 percent to 18 percent during the same period.

Interregional comparisons

Proulx and Cauchy report on a comparison of interprovincial shipments of manufactured goods and shipments of primary and secondary goods to the U.S. by using results from Proulx's recent study for the Borderlands Group. The most important finding is that Quebec's shipments to the U.S. increased much more rapidly than to other provinces. They conclude that Quebec's economic space has evolved to reflect a north-south orientation which is more dynamic and less artificial than the east-west axis. Quebec interprovincial shipments of manufactured goods increased only 2.9 percent on average from 1974 to 1984, whereas international exports increased 14.7 percent. Proulx and Cauchy examine in detail the 75 percent of Quebec exports that go to bordering regions of the U.S., particularly several New England states, where Quebec exports are increasing most rapidly. Proulx and Cauchy contend that the challenge for Quebec is to diversify its exports because the markets of Canada and the United States are less dynamic.

Comparison of the impact of interprovincial and international trade on the Quebec economy

Proulx and Cauchy report estimates of the impact of international and interprovincial trade on the Quebec economy using the Quebec Bureau of Statistics input-output model. They conclude that international exports are more profitable than interprovincial. Dollar-per-dollar they produce more employment income, more value added, more provincial and federal government revenue. They also argue that, while they generate slightly less employment, in the longer run employment in competitive international scale export industries represents a better bet on the future than employment in protected industries focused on domestic markets. This is incontestable. The problem is how it can be accomplished. On this Proulx and Cauchy are silent.

Services

Proulx and Cauchy examine trade in commercial services using unpublished data provided by Statistics Canada which have been regionalized based on the location of the head office. Payments and receipts of these services are concentrated in Ontario and Quebec. Consulting engineers and consulting services are the principal industries responsible for Quebec's surplus of commercial services. Quebec has half of the employees of exporting consulting engineering firms. Quebec is way ahead in foreign fees. Proulx and Cauchy observe that the economic aggregates are more sensitive to exports of commercial services than exports in general.

Conclusions

Proulx and Cauchy conclude that if the trade balances of various goods are examined to ascertain the comparative advantage of Quebec, positive balances in international trade would be found for airplane motors and parts, telecommunications equipment and material, and aircraft parts. Surprisingly, they do not mention the positive balances in paper and allied products and primary metals, leaving the impression that Quebec's comparative advantage is in high tech products. They omit the other products because they confine their analysis to the fifteen most important products.

In interprovincial trade, Proulx and Cauchy report that positive balances are found for hats and clothing, wood, and paper and allied products. In their view, the surpluses in these sectors are in the process of disappearing following the Canada-U.S. Free Trade Agreement. The strength of Quebec in paper and allied products and primary metals is expected to continue even in a period of political and economic transition.

Proulx and Cauchy claim that it is necessary to go beyond trade balances to establish the comparative advantage of Quebec. New theories of international trade which take into account market imperfections, economies of scale, and efforts to capture rents and externalities using subsidies should be considered, subject of course to the constraints of GATT and the Free Trade Agreement. Considerable analysis is necessary to clarify the economic policy for a confederal or sovereign Quebec. They end their paper with a plea for more research on Quebec trade to guide policies for innovation, research and development, and education and training. While they offer no concrete proposals, they definitely come down on the side of an active industrial policy for Quebec to improve its trade position. In so doing, they overlook the extent to which such policies have been tried and found wanting in the past.

Study 4

"The Question of Employment in Quebec: the Photo and the Film," by Pierre Fortin

(Commission, 1991b, pp.167-241)

General

Pierre Fortin's study is a useful survey of the Quebec labour market, which he also uses as a vehicle to provide some of his own views on incomes policy and monetary union. Its perspective is largely comparative, with Ontario being the main focus, providing many interesting and revealing comparisons.

The body of Fortin's study has two main parts: the first, the photo, provides a snapshot of the Quebec labour market in 1989 (or 1988 in certain cases); the second, the film, explores the evolution of the Quebec labour market over a longer period starting in the 1960s, focusing on the factors underlying the increase in the gap between the unemployment rate in Quebec and Ontario.

It is only in his conclusion that Fortin's sovereigntist leanings become apparent. He also advocates his personal prescriptions for stabilization policy and offers his optimistic speculations on the Quebec labour market in the 1990s. In contrast, the earlier sections of the study are more descriptive and analytical and draw on Fortin's extensive research on the causes of structural unemployment in Quebec.

Overall, there is little—if anything—in this study which could be viewed as undermining the federalist cause. Indeed, much of the material provided underlines the relative weakness of the Quebec labour market. Although Fortin does not emphasize the financial difficulties a sovereign Quebec could face, his material could be used by federalists to make a convincing case that weaknesses in the Quebec labour market would be exacerbated by sovereignty and would impede adjustment to the economic restructuring likely to be necessitated by sovereignty.

The photo

This section of the study is primarily descriptive and cannot be seriously faulted. Fortin relies mainly on data from the labour force survey to profile the state of the Quebec labour market in 1989 (or 1988), supplemented by comparable data for the U.S. and other countries where necessary. Even in a good year, such as 1988, Quebec had one of the highest unemployment rates in North America, surpassed only by the Atlantic provinces, and British Columbia in Canada and by Louisiana and West Virginia in the United States. He also notes that Montreal has the highest unemployment rate of urban agglomerations of more than 200,000 people.

Quebec ranks as one of the worst areas in North America in the creation of jobs. In particularly damning terms, Fortin calls this the Achilles heel of the Quebec economy. Compared to Ontario, Quebec had a deficit of 430,000 employees in 1989 on account of higher unemployment and lower labour force participation. Data on gross flows are used to show that people are unemployed more frequently and longer in Quebec than in Ontario.

Fortin shows that the industrial distribution of employment is similar in Quebec and Ontario, but that Quebec's distribution is more concentrated in the traditional sectors of textiles, clothing, wood, and paper while Ontario's is more concentrated in industries related to the production of motor vehicles. Workers' levels of education reveal striking gaps: workers with less than a grade nine education account for 24 percent of labour force in Quebec compared to 14 percent in Ontario, and workers with a university degree account for only 10.5 percent of the labour force in Quebec compared to 13.5 percent in Ontario. That this education gap has increased over the last ten years is not mentioned. The obvious point that Quebec needs to invest more in human capital is made. The extent to which the labour force participation of women in Quebec (62 percent) falls behind that in the United States (66 percent), and Ontario (71 percent) is emphasized.

The film

In this section, Fortin presents descriptive material on the labour market, but he goes beyond this to analyze labour market trends. He analyses the increase in the Quebec unemployment rate from 1.8 percent in 1948 to 9.3 percent in 1989, the increase in the gap between the Quebec and Ontario unemployment rates from 1 percentage point to 3.75 percentage points after the 1981 to 1982 recession, and the increase in the Quebec-Ontario gap in the employment population ratio from 30 employees per 1,000 persons after World War II to 80 employees since 1983. The paradox of the outward shift in the vacancy-unemployment relationship in the 1970s and 1980s is cited.

Five factors are offered by Fortin to explain the outward drift in the vacancy-unemployment relationship and the increase in structural unemployment:

1) the demographic congestion caused by the entry of baby-boomers and women into the labour force;

2) the increased generosity of unemployment insurance;

3) higher salaries in construction and the public sector, and the increase in the minimum wage and related spillover effects on other sectors;

4) profound structural change in the Quebec economy;

5) the persistence of unemployment caused by the continuing battle against inflation.

The first four of these factors are the standard ones cited in the empirical literature on the determinants of structural unemployment. Fortin himself has contributed significantly to this literature, providing his own quantitative estimates of the importance of these factors in earlier studies which he cites. His assessment of the importance of at least the first three of these factors would be accepted by most analysts. The fact that the first three factors caused a significant increase in the Quebec unemployment rate, and that the increase has since largely reversed, is widely recognized.

In contrast, Fortin's fifth factor and his discussion of its overwhelming relative importance in explaining the increase in structural unemployment in Quebec and in the Quebec-Ontario gap would not be accepted by most macroeconomists, particularly those at the Bank of Canada and the Department of Finance. They would argue that there is a Non-Accelerating Inflation Rate of Unemployment (NAIRU) below which the unemployment rate cannot go without giving rise to accelerating inflation. The unemployment rate in 1989, which is the reference year for Fortin's analysis, is believed to be below the NAIRU because of the increasing inflationary pressures that were manifest and is thus not sustainable. For Fortin's fifth factor to be valid, the rate of unemployment has to be above the NAIRU.

Another factor not mentioned by Fortin is the lesser mobility of Quebec labour because of language and culture. If changes occur which affect employment, such as technological change or an increase in trade, a province such as Quebec with a less mobile labour force will experience a greater increase in structural unemployment.

Fortin's discussion of the first factor of demographic congestion is good. He estimates that, at the height of the demographic bulge at the end of the 1970s, the high unemployment rate of youth raised the overall unemployment rate by 1.5 percentage points. His assessment that the increased participation of women has not raised the unemployment rate since the rate of unemployment of women and men is similar is uncontestable. Finally, his view that the impact of demographic congestion in raising the unemployment rate through the 1970s was reversed in the 1980s is generally accepted.

Fortin's treatment of the second factor of unemployment insurance is informative. His calculation of the increase in the implicit subsidy rate of unemployment insurance in Quebec from 30 percent to 330 percent as a result of the 1971 unemployment insurance changes and the subsequent decline from 194 percent to 109 percent as a result of the 1989 reforms is striking. Fortin cites the range of estimates of an increase in the unemployment rate of 0.5 to 1.5 percentage points for the 1971 unemployment insurance changes with his own estimate of 0.7 percent at the bottom end of the range. In my view, the rise in average unemployment rates after 1971 makes the high end of the range more likely.

Fortin makes five telling observations on the impact of unemployment insurance:

1) the 1971 changes came just before the shift out in the vacancy-unemployment relationship and the increase in the unemployment rate;

2) the 1971 change provided a large incentive to join the labour force just before the big increase in the participation rate;

3) the implicit subsidy rate increased in Quebec (330 percent) more than in Ontario (230 percent);

4) the unemployment rate in the U.S. where there was no increase in unemployment insurance did not rise as in Canada;

5) the 1989 unemployment insurance reform which lowered the implicit subsidy rate to 110 percent should have a negative effect on the participation rate and unemployment rate.

On the third factor of the salary increase, Fortin observes that between 1966 and 1979 salaries in construction and the public sector increased much more rapidly than in other sectors in Quebec and the corresponding sectors in Ontario. He estimates that salaries in these two sectors, which account for 25 percent of Quebec employees, were raised artificially by 5 percent in 1980 which in turn increased salaries in the rest of the economy by 2 percent. The total economy-wide increase was thus around 3 percent. Assuming an elasticity of demand for labour of .5 percent, he estimates that the salary increase would reduce employment by 1.5 percent or 8 employees per thousand persons over fifteen years of age. However, as Fortin notes, the increase in salaries was reversed by the recession of 1981 and 1982 so it does not help to explain the deterioration in the Quebec labour market. Similarly, Fortin estimates that the large increase in the minimum wage in the 1960s and the early 1970s caused an increase in the unemployment rate of youths of 2 to 3 percentage points, but was also reversed.

On the fourth factor of structural change, Fortin emphasizes the profound structural changes which the Quebec economy has undergone and which have narrowed the productivity gap with Ontario from around 15 percent in the late 1960s to about 5 percent in recent years. These structural changes involved a movement out of the traditional mining sector, the manufacturing sectors of leather, textiles and clothing, and maritime transport into the modern durable goods sector (metal fabrication, transportation equipment, machinery, and electrical products) and services (consulting engineering, computer services, transportation, communications and finance). Fortin also mentions the exodus of the anglophone economic elite of Montreal as being an important change. Fortin does not offer any quantitative estimates of the impact of structural change on the Quebec unemployment rate. He also does not discuss how the problems of structural change can be exacerbated by Quebec's relatively immobile labour force.

Concerning the fifth factor of the impact of the battle against inflation, Fortin's discussion is unsatisfactory. He presents no convincing evidence of the importance of hysteresis (the tendency of any increase in the unemployment rate for whatever reason to become the normal operating level of the economy after enough time has elapsed). He also makes a puzzling statement that the phenomenon of hysteresis is symmetric by which he means that a prolonged period of low unemployment at the cost of slightly higher inflation would melt away the hard core of inactivity, instability and poverty. This flies in the face of the opinions of most macroeconomists who no longer accept the existence of a permanent trade-off between unemployment and inflation.

Fortin's discussion of the five factors behind the increase in the unemployment rate in Quebec does not really resolve the issue to my satisfaction. As he points out, the first three factors were largely reversed, so they do not explain the persistence of the increase. Of the last two factors, neither of which Fortin was able to quantify in his study, only structural change seems to be relevant. The puzzle thus remains. Why did the rate of unemployment in Quebec go up so much more than in Ontario?

Conclusion

Besides summarizing the conclusions of his review of the Quebec labour market, Fortin puts forwards his views on Quebec labour markets in the 1990s. He expects that during the 1990s unemployment will decline progressively in Quebec. His view is based on several factors: the productivity catch up is over; the demographics will remain favourable to the employment of youth; social programs will be stabilized; and the realism of salaries and prices will persist as workers and firms gain a better understanding of the benefits of security and competitiveness. Fortin's analysis of prospects for labour markets in the 1990s is only impressionistic and not very systematic. It is not based on consistent long-term projections for the Quebec economy. Such projections would have to be conditional on a number of key assumptions, including the constitutional status of Quebec. It is notable that Fortin does not mention the possibility that the disruptions resulting from the accession to sovereignty could result in a deterioration of the Quebec labour market.

In his conclusion, Fortin also expresses his views on some topics which are not really fully developed in the body. First, he presents his own policy prescriptions for concerted action to restrain salaries and prices. Fortin argues that Quebec has benefitted from a form of spontaneous direct action on salaries and prices. To support this, he cites the more moderate increase in wages and prices in Quebec since 1982. In my view, this neglects the fact that some of the recent settlements with low wage increases such as the those for the public service, Quebec-Hydro and construction were imposed by the government. It also ignores an equally plausible and more simple explanation that the greater degree of wage restraint simply represents the impact of the greater degree of slack in Quebec labour markets over the period. Fortin believes that community spirit in Quebec would enhance the prospects for voluntary wage restraint. Fortin also argues that the countries with the best performance such as Japan, Germany, Sweden, Switzerland, Norway, and Austria are all countries that practice concertation among the social partners. Another interpretation, which I find to be more plausible, is that countries which create the best economic climate through anti-inflationary monetary policies such as Japan, Germany, Switzerland, and Austria are ones which have the best economic performance.

Second, Fortin argues that a monetary union is imperative for Quebec. In his view, this imperative is based on the integration of Quebec with Canada and the United States. His preference is for a fixed exchange rate tied to a weighted average of the Canadian and U.S. dollars which would be revised as the trade shares of Quebec evolved. But this is not really a proposal for a monetary union. There would still be transaction costs when changing from Quebec dollars to either Canadian or U.S. dollars, and there would still be a risk of a change of parity. Fortin's discussion of monetary union is really inconsistent with his much better and more thorough discussion of the monetary options of a sovereign Quebec.

Third, Fortin tries to integrate his proposal for concertation with a monetary union in arguing that the only possible way to achieve full employment without inflation would be wage and price restraint based on a fair and flexible inflation target. He claims that this is the only form of independent monetary policy open to Quebec.

Study 5

"International Financial Integration and the Political Interdependence of National Macroeconomic Policies," by Daniel Racette

(Commission, 1991b, pp.243-282)

Daniel Racette's study is a good survey of the implications of integrated international financial markets for the ability of a sovereign Quebec government to conduct an independent monetary policy. It should help to pour cold water on the enthusiasm of Quebec nationalists who see sovereignty as a way to escape from the financial discipline imposed by the Bank of Canada.

Racette asks the critical question of the scope for independent national stabilization policies in a context of increasing globalization of markets. His thoughtful answer is that international competition imposes major constraints on macroeconomic policies and forces governments to exercise discipline in the use of these instruments. In the first part of the study, he examines the characteristics and consequences of the international integration of financial markets. In the second part, he considers the situation in the major industrialized countries in order to ascertain the context in which monetary and fiscal policy in North America will have to operate. In the third part, he presents his conclusions concerning the discipline imposed on governments in the conduct of their monetary and fiscal policy.

The integration of capital markets: phenomena and consequences

Racette argues that since the 1970s the international integration of international finance has developed greatly as a result of progress in communications and computers and the deregulation and opening up of national financial markets. The deregulation has included the breaking down of the barriers between different types of financial institutions, the dismantling of exchange controls, the opening up of markets to foreign financial institutions, the creation of "offshore markets," and the creation of many new and more flexible financial instruments. These changes all served to increase the mobility of capital and to improve the allocation of world-wide savings.

Racette contends that, as expected, the increasing integration has resulted in a closer correspondence between movements in real interest rates over the course of the last decade than over the two preceding decades. He also notes that different countries have different risk premiums for their interest rates. In 1989 Japan became the country with the lowest real interest rate of the Group of Seven. The United States and Canada have generally had to pay a risk premium in relation to Germany and Japan in recent years. The risk premiums result from the existence of sovereign governments with their own independent monetary, fiscal and taxation policy.

According to Racette, the risk premium can be divided into three parts. The first part is related to taxation and regulation. Investors seek after-tax rates of return which are higher than they can get in their own markets. Racette considers this part to be relatively unimportant because of the harmonization of tax policies. The second part is tied to the independence of fiscal policy. Governments can rely too heavily on deficit spending and impose a credit risk on their national borrowers. Racette reports that it has not been possible to identify empirically such an effect for industrialized countries. The third part of the premium reflects the independence of monetary policy. Since an independent monetary policy can lead to higher inflation and a depreciation of the exchange rate. Investors must take such an eventuality into account in assessing risk. By assessing these three types of risk and by determining the interest rate of a particular country, financial markets impose a price for not following disciplined macroeconomic policies.

The current situation in the major industrialized countries

Racette examines the experience of countries with what he considers undisciplined policies—namely the United States, Canada, and the United Kingdom—and those with disciplined policies—Germany and Japan.

2) a Quebec currency with a fixed exchange rate in terms of the Canadian dollar (pseudo-monetary union with Canada);

3) a Quebec currency with a fixed exchange rate in terms of the U.S. dollar (pseudo-monetary union with the United States);

4) a Quebec currency with a floating exchange rate.

The common currency option would require Quebec legislation decreeing that Canadian money was legal tender in Quebec. Regulations for financial institutions would also need to be harmonized. Fortin envisages two possible scenarios for the institutional framework for the formulation of a common monetary policy. In the first, a supranational Quebec-Canada Council would replace the Board of Directors and Executive Committee of the Bank of Canada and policy could be conducted decentrally through Canadian and Quebec central banks. A formula would have to be negotiated on the sharing of the central bank profits (seigniorage).

Fortin compares his proposal for sharing authority over monetary policy to the Federal Reserve System of the United States with its board, open market committee and regional banks. He also cites the Monetary Union of West Africa and the proposed European community (excluding the U.K.) system for the year 2000 as examples of such a system. He neglects to point out important differences and problems. The Federal Reserve System answers to only one political authority, the United States government. The West African and proposed European systems involve the participation of many states of comparable economic and political weight. The proposed Canadian system would involve only two partners and one would be three times the size of the other. In addition, it is quite possible that the separation of Quebec could engender such a backlash in the rest of Canada that it would be impossible to reach an agreement.

That Canada could refuse to share authority over monetary policy is acknowledged by Fortin. In this case, he argues, Quebec could always opt for something like the status quo. Quebec could still use Canadian money and leave the Bank of Canada to formulate the monetary policy of the monetary union. Quebec banks could continue to hold their reserves as deposits with the Bank of Canada. Fortin argues that the reserves and currency would be, in effect, debt of the Canadian government on which no interest was paid. As such, it would be a disguised tax that would increase the profits of the Bank of Canada. While Canada might object to particular formulas for profit sharing, there would be a critical share above which it would be in Canada's interest to agree to the proposal. Fortin cites the case of Ireland, which, after its independence from the United Kingdom in 1921, continued to use the pound sterling until 1928.

Fortin presents this option as if Canada would have no choice but to go along with it. Yet, if Canada did not agree, it would be relatively simple to prevent Quebec from using Canadian currency as legal tender. Canada could refuse to provide Quebec with the needed supplies of coin and currency. Canada could introduce a law which prevents individuals from taking more than a certain amount of currency outside of the country. The United States already has a law requiring that currency above a certain amount taken out of the country must be declared. If Quebec were to introduce its own coins and currency, there would no longer be a pure monetary union, but a fixed exchange rate system. Canada would not have to allow Quebec financial institutions to hold reserves at the Bank of Canada. Canada could prevent Canadian financial institutions from acting as clearing agencies for Quebec financial institutions. It is misleading to create the impression that a monetary union could result from a unilateral decision of Quebec. Canada would have to agree for the system to be workable for Quebec. Such agreement could be expected only if other outstanding issues, such as trade and the division of the public debt, were settled to Canada's satisfaction.

The second and third option of fixed exchange rate pegged to the Canadian dollar would require the creation of a Quebec central bank. Monetary policy would have to be conducted so as to preserve the fixed parity.

Under the fourth option of a floating exchange rate, the degree of flexibility could be greater or less and would be influenced by the intervention of the central bank on the foreign exchange market and by the monetary and fiscal policy adopted by the government.

The costs of a separate currency for Quebec

Fortin discusses the three traditional functions of money, as a unit of account, medium of exchange, and store of value. He emphasizes that the advantage of a money as a social institution depends on the size of the economic and geographic area within which it is utilized. He identifies three types of costs in Quebec-Canada transactions: 1) transaction costs stemming from the need to convert currencies, 2) accounting costs from the necessity to calculate prices in Canadian and Quebec currency, and 3) costs of risk and uncertainty associated with unexpected fluctuations in the exchange rate. He acknowledges that while it is difficult to quantify these costs, the costs are not negligible. They would be minimized under option two of the fixed exchange rate and be much higher in option four of the floating exchange rate.

The annual additional accounting and transaction costs resulting from the use of separate currencies in the European Community is around 1 percent of GDP. Fortin estimates that, taking account of the relative magnitude of Quebec trade, the additional costs of a separate currency in Quebec would be 0.6 percent of GDP—one billion dollars in 1990. Using a 5 percent real interest rate and a 2.5 percent long-term growth rate for Quebec, he estimates that the present value of the additional costs would be $40 billion, a far from negligible figure. Canada would also experience considerable additional costs if Quebec were to introduce a separate currency.

But the estimate of the additional costs of a separate currency for Quebec provided by Fortin is only the roughest of figures. Fortin does not even explain the basis of his calculation. Much more work would be required before any confidence could be attached to his estimate.

Fortin cites evidence from recent studies to show that future markets in currency only protect imperfectly against exchange risk and involve significant transaction costs. He argues that exchange risk is thus translated into an increase in transaction costs and into risk premiums in interest rates. This represents not only static costs, but also dynamic costs, with negative effects on economic growth. In the longer run, increases in interest rates reduce the stock of physical and human capital in the economy.

Fortin also argues that increased transaction costs cause inefficiencies in the same way that imposing tariffs does. It would be difficult, he argues, to have a common market without a monetary union.

The benefits of a separate currency for Quebec

In his discussion of the benefits of a separate Quebec currency, Fortin distinguishes between the transition period and the long run. Fortin argues that in the transition period Quebec would have to have a stable exchange rate to gain confidence in the new Quebec currency. There would thus not be much room for an autonomous monetary policy. A separate currency for Quebec would entail costs, but bring no benefits other than information on monetary aggregates.

Fortin considers the advantages of a separate currency once confidence is established. Fluctuations in the exchange rate can absorb asymmetric shocks which affect the economy, but, he argues, this advantage should not be exaggerated in the case of a small open economy such as Quebec.

Fortin argues that it is necessary to have an adequate understanding of the role and limits of monetary policy. When monetary policy is credible and fully anticipated and with full indexing, it does not have a significant impact on the standard of living, but only on inflation. He also warns that an expansionary monetary policy will raise—not lower—interest rates. It is only when monetary policy is not credible and can fool expectations that it can have an impact on the real sector of the economy. Fortin concludes that because of subjective and volatile variables, it is impossible to predict the impact of monetary policy.

Fortin cites the weak relation between the rate of growth of money and real GDP as evidence of money's lack of real impact. The only time money growth had a strong impact on real activity was in 1981, 1982, and again in 1990 because of the lack of credibility of monetary policy during those years. He argues that the objective of monetary policy should be limited to long-run price stability, which requires the establishment of clear and credible objectives defined in terms of the growth of the monetary aggregates.

While I share Fortin's long run objective for monetary policy, I think that the short run conduct of monetary policy is much more difficult than he suggests. In particular, I do not believe that we can rely completely on monetary aggregates as indicators of monetary policy. A much more eclectic approach which takes into account a wider range of economic indicators including interest rates, real activity, the unemployment rate, wage and price trends, and even the stability of the financial system is required. This approach is followed by the Bank of Canada.

Concerning the role of monetary policy in government finance, Fortin makes the valid point that financing government deficits by printing money is equivalent to a tax on the holders of government debt. He argues that such a tax is inefficient and undemocratic.

According to Fortin, an independent monetary policy would enable Quebec to have a more stable and less inflationary monetary policy than that of the Bank of Canada. But inflation has been relatively low in Canada since 1983 and, to the extent the anti-inflationary policy of the Bank of Canada is pursued and becomes more credible, it will be possible in the long run to achieve a reduction in inflation without an increase in unemployment. Fortin acknowledges that, while it is possible for Quebec to pursue a less inflationary monetary policy, it is not certain.

The other possible advantage for Quebec of a floating exchange rate would be to allow an adjustment in the external value of the currency in response to external shocks such as changes in demand for exports. Fortin distinguishes between shocks that affect the Quebec and Canadian economies similarly and differently. He argues that devaluing currency in response to similar shock would be an attempt to export unemployment to Canada, which could lead to self-defeating reprisals.

On the other hand, Fortin argues that a depreciation in response to a shock which only reduces the demand for Quebec exports could facilitate the process of adjustment of Quebec's real exchange rate in the face of nominal wage rigidities. This could reduce any temporary unemployment created by the shock. The advantage of exchange rate adjustment would depend on the availability of alternative methods of adjustment. Fortin cites with approval a Bank of Canada study which shows that the terms of exchange between Canadian regions are already quite flexible. Furthermore, the mobility of factors, especially labour, can mitigate the impact of any shock.

Fortin fails to make the case that the limited mobility of francophone Quebec labour implies a greater role for exchange rate fluctuations in fostering adjustment in Quebec than in the rest of Canada where labour is more mobile.

Fortin's overall conclusion on the benefits of a separate currency for Quebec is that they are limited to a certain autonomy in carrying out anti-inflationary policies and in using of the exchange rate to increase the rapidity of adjustment to external shocks.

Monetary union with the United States

Fortin asks whether a monetary union or pseudo-union with the United States would be preferable to one with Canada. In response, he makes six points:

1) Monetary union goes along with a common market. In spite of free trade, Quebec is far from having a common market with the U.S.

2) Quebec has a much higher volume of transactions with Canada.

3) The transition costs of a monetary union with the U.S. would be greater than the costs of a union with Canada.

4) Quebec is more likely to experience shocks which do not affect the United States than those which do not affect Canada.

5) It is possible that Quebec would have experienced less inflation since 1980 if it had been in a monetary union with the United States, but it is necessary to determine if Quebec was subjected to more inflationary shocks during that period.

6) Some have suggested that a monetary union with the United States would result in lower interest rates for Quebec, but the interest rates are similar if one accounts for exchange rate expectations.

Fortin interprets these points as favouring a Quebec-Canada monetary union.

Conclusion

Fortin's conclusion is that a pure monetary union with Canada is the most advantageous option for a sovereign Quebec since it will simplify calculations and help to preserve the integration of markets. This option would be most advantageous for Canada to avoid an increase in the costs of exchange with Quebec. While sovereigntists may see this as an argument in favour of sovereignty-association, it is an even stronger argument in favour of a continuation of a federalist system given the uncertainty of a continued monetary union if Quebec were to separate.

The cost to Quebec of not running an autonomous monetary policy and not floating its exchange rate are regarded by Fortin as of limited importance, particularly since the external shocks facing Quebec are likely to be shared with Canada. He neglects to mention the adjustment problems caused by the lesser degree of labour mobility in Quebec.

Fortin does not see much justification for a fixed exchange rate with Canada. It would introduce transaction costs and exchange rate risk. Its only advantage is that statistics could be collected on the financial flows and stocks for Quebec. He regards this option as a fall-back position if Quebec and Canada could not agree on a monetary union.

The option of a fixed rate pegged to the U.S. dollar is considered to be viable by Fortin. But he sees it as less advantageous to Quebec than a fixed rate pegged to the Canadian dollar because of the lesser volume of trade and greater dissimilarities between the two economies.

Fortin does raise the interesting possibility that a North American monetary block with a common currency could become the preferred monetary option in the near future, thereby favouring the development of a real North American Common market. Fortin's rather convincing discussion of the benefits of a monetary union between Quebec and Canada also suggests that a Canada-U.S. monetary union would be beneficial from an economic point of view. The politics of such a monetary union would, of course, be another story. But, in any event, a North American monetary union is much more likely if Quebec remains part of Canada then at least two of the three possible partners are already using the same currency. A movement to monetary integration is not likely to be best served by a breakup of Canada.

Study 7

"An Analysis Of The Fiscal And Budgetary Activities Of The Federal Government: The Evolution And Interprovincial Comparisons," By The Secretariat

(Commission, 1991b, pp.303-352)

This study, prepared by the secretariat of the commission, provides estimates of the interprovincial breakdown of federal government expenditures, revenues and budget balances for the five Canadian regions. These data are frequently used indicators of the costs and benefits of Confederation. The secretariat utilizes the data from the provincial economic accounts because they are the only available data broken down by province. The data cover the 1961 to 1988 period. The secretariat also makes comparisons with fiscal balance data provided to the Commission by the Desjardin movement, the Parti Québécois, the Conseil du Patronat du Québec, the Association des Économistes Québécois, and other studies.

Methodology

The secretariat makes some adjustments to the provincial accounts data to eliminate certain biases in the data:

- Federal sales tax, excise taxes and customs duties are reallocated on the basis of consumption rather than production.
- Investment income is excluded since it does not reflect obligatory tax revenue, but voluntary transactions.
- Public debt charges are excluded because they reflect voluntary transactions.
- Tax point transfers are treated as fiscal transfers.
- Oil import subsidies and export taxes are eliminated to facilitate comparisons with provinces which benefitted from the federal government's regulation of oil prices.

In my view, all of these adjustments except the last are reasonable. As for the last, it would have been more reasonable to include the implicit subsidies resulting from regulated oil prices in the fiscal balances. The approach chosen by the commission substantially underestimates the magnitude of the transfers from the Prairie region to the rest of Canada, thereby underestimating Quebec's fiscal benefits from 1973 to 1985, when oil prices were regulated. Also not allocating federal government expenditures abroad to the provinces should be a source of slight bias.

From a methodological point of view, one of the main differences from other approaches is that no explicit adjustment is made to eliminate the deficit. Instead, the adjustments themselves tend to reduce the magnitude of the deficit and the adjusted corrected balances are compared with the national average. This is, in effect, an implicit adjustment for the deficit.

Expenditures

The secretariat analyses the distribution of each major category of federal spending separately. Quebec has always benefitted least from federal expenditures on goods and services in spite of the National Capital Region's presence in Quebec. A recent study by the Council of Atlantic Premiers confirmed that Quebec is the province in which federal employment creation expenditures have been the lowest. Another recent study by the Quebec Ministry of Industry, Commerce and Technology concluded that, in taking account of total research and development expenditures, Quebec and Alberta had a negative balance.

In spite of its high share of unemployment insurance benefits, Quebec's share of transfers to persons is only the same in 1988 as its population share. The secretariat attributes this to the under-representation in Quebec of individuals eligible for family allowances and of veterans and public servants in receipt of pensions. The improvement in Quebec since the mid-1960s can be explained by the increase in old age pensions resulting from the greater numbers of old age pensioners in the Quebec population and from the introduction of the Guaranteed Income Supplement.

The secretariat notes that Quebec maintained its population share of transfers to business from 1967 to 1981, but since 1981 Quebec's share has fallen sharply and has not gone above 60 percent of the national average. As an equalization-receiving province, Quebec has received a share of fiscal transfers to governments above its demographic weight and about 25 percent above the national average.

The secretariat concludes that Quebec's share of federal expenditures has been systematically below its demographic weight since 1961 except for the years 1978, 1980 and 1983. But in my view, two additional points are worth noting. First, from 1978 to 1983, Quebec's shares are very close to the national average. Second, shares of expenditure are not as good an indicator of the benefit Quebec derives from the federal government as the fiscal balance, which also takes into account revenues, is.

Budget balances

From 1961 to 1974, the secretariat states, the federal government was able to maintain its corrected budget balance at the national level in a surplus position. From 1974 to 1978, inflation increased spending more than revenues and caused a major swing into deficit. From 1979 to 1981, the federal government was able to bring its position back towards balance. The 1982 recession turned the situation around again and produced an unprecedented deficit by 1984. Fiscal restraint after 1984 brought the deficit back to surplus by 1988.

The per capita fiscal gain estimated by the secretariat for the five Canadian regions in relation to the national average is shown in table 7. Figure 1 provides a graph of the same information.

According to the secretariat, the data demonstrate that until the end of the 1960s, Quebec contributed proportionally more than other regions to the redistributional activities of the federal government, registering a net loss per capita of between $17 and $163. The situation reversed in 1968, after which Quebec recorded a net fiscal gain which steadily increased from $55 per capita in 1969 to $818 in 1982 (still well below the gain of the Atlantic provinces). The economic recovery after 1983 and federal fiscal restraint reduced the net gain substantially to $409 in 1988. The 1988 net gain per capita is 40 percent less than that of the Prairies and only one eighth of that of the Atlantic provinces. According to the secretariat, these results confirm other studies' results—that Quebec was a net contributor to fiscal federalism in the 1960s but a net beneficiary from the beginning of the 1970s, with a significant reduction in benefits since 1983.

Two points are worth making about the secretariat's estimates and conclusions. First, by excluding the oil import subsidy and export tax and the related transfers from the Prairies to the rest of Canada (which kept the domestic price of oil below the world price from 1973 to 1985), the secretariat ignores a massive transfer to Quebec mandated by federal government policy. At its peak in 1981, this transfer was worth $5 to $6 billion or approximately $800 per capita. Second, the secretariat fails to mention the large absolute magnitude of the transfers in 1988. A net fiscal gain of $409 per capita in 1988 is $2.7 billion dollars, a substantial amount by anyone's reckoning.

Limits of the analysis

The secretariat warns that fiscal analysis does not shed light on the global regional incidence of all federal economic interventions. Nor does fiscal analysis reveal what the impact on Quebec public finances would be of taking over federal revenues and expenditures in the event of sovereignty. And fiscal analysis reveals nothing about the advantages all regions of Canada derive from sharing economic space.

TABLE 7

PER CAPITA FISCAL GAIN GAP IN RELATION TO THE NATIONAL AVERAGE

Year	Gap				
	Atlantic	Quebec	Ontario	Prairies	B.C.
1961	$1,067	($163)	($286)	$227	($64)
1962	$1,103	($153)	($260)	$256	($256)
1963	$1,125	($119)	($268)	$207	($264)
1964	$1,180	($64)	($316)	$197	($316)
1965	$1,302	($17)	($386)	$224	($344)
1966	$1,364	($40)	($344)	$186	($372)
1967	$1,542	$0	($368)	$114	($436)
1968	$1,634	$55	($440)	$143	($473)
1969	$1,775	$133	($515)	$203	($627)
1970	$1,605	$141	($509)	$221	($503)
1971	$1,751	$230	($580)	$224	($593)
1972	$1,839	$276	($611)	$193	($626)
1973	$1,998	$302	($606)	$161	($786)
1974	$2,164	$379	($609)	($74)	($734)
1975	$2,243	$386	($453)	($532)	($641)
1976	$2,476	$353	($460)	($586)	($639)
1977	$2,687	$396	($501)	($678)	($631)
1978	$2,773	$522	($610)	($621)	($702)
1979	$2,626	$490	($545)	($586)	($738)
1980	$2,719	$498	($471)	($753)	($778)
1981	$2,853	$670	($443)	($1,130)	($762)
1982	$2,969	$818	($535)	($1,387)	($459)
1983	$3,092	$754	($686)	($1,113)	($333)
1984	$3,302	$675	($807)	($936)	($209)
1985	$3,510	$631	($897)	($825)	($139)
1986	$3,406	$447	($1,199)	$144	($136)
1987	$3,138	$366	($1,290)	$693	($254)
1988	$3,271	$409	($1,337)	$687	($231)

Note: A number in parenthesis indicates a fiscal gain inferior to the national average.

Source: Commission sur l'avenir politique et constitutionnel du Québec (1991b, p.335).

FIGURE 1

CORRECTED BUDGETARY BALANCE GAP IN RELATION TO THE NATIONAL AVERAGE

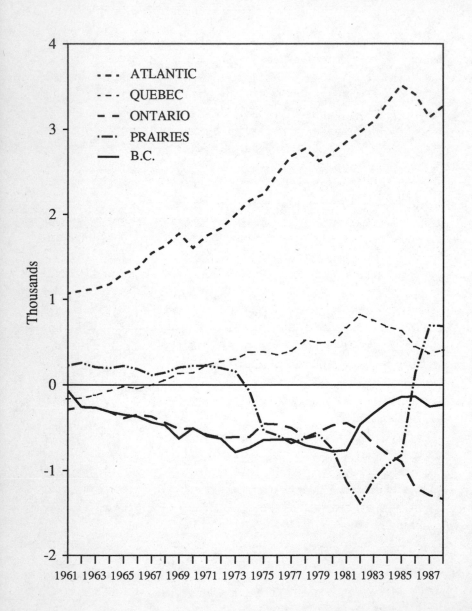

Study 8

"The Presence of the Federal Government in Quebec: Federal Transfer Programs to the Provinces, the Functioning and Recent Evolution," by the Ministry of Finance of Quebec

(Commission, 1991b, pp.353-391)

Prepared by the Quebec Ministry of Finance, this study provides background information on the importance to Quebec of federal transfer programs to the provinces. The first five sections of the study provide a brief description of the programs accompanied by tables and graphs presenting the financial data. The final section, which is of most interest, raises some problems with the programs from the point of view of the Quebec government operating within the current federal structure. The ministry's study does not address the broader issues of the relevance of federal transfers for the desirability of renewed federalism or sovereignty.

The ministry lists the most important federal transfer programs, such as the established programs financing, equalization, and the Canada Assistance Plan, which transferred $4.6 billion, $3.7 billion, and $1.7 billion respectively to Quebec in 1989-90. The total amount of federal transfers received by Quebec in 1989-90 was $10.6 billion out of total federal transfers of $35.2 billion. Federal transfers to Quebec have stagnated since 1983-84, falling from 28.9 percent of GDP in 1983-84 to 21.6 percent in 1989-90. But I find these data misleading because they include only cash transfers and ignore the transfer of tax points which form a larger part of the transfer programs for Quebec than the other provinces because of opting out. The value of these tax points has been steadily increasing.

According to the study 43 percent of the transfers go to the three wealthiest provinces and only 57 percent to the remaining seven provinces, including Quebec. Because Quebec receives an extra 16.5 percent abatement of personal income tax points, the study's authors argue, the portion of cash transfers is less important in Quebec than in other provinces.

The Quebec Ministry of Finance discusses the financing of the Established Programs Financing Program, which provides funding for health and post-secondary education and reviews the evolution of transfers. It presents the formula for the total federal contribution ($212.65 in 1975-76, which is indexed annually according to the evolution of GNP, taking into account some limitations in specific years, and then multiplied by the Quebec population) and the subtraction of tax points. The study provides estimates of the impact of federal cutbacks in established programs financing from 1982-83 to 1990-91. The cumulative impact of the cuts was estimated to be $14.6 billion for Canada and $3.8 billion for Quebec. In 1990-91 alone the cuts were estimated to be $5.1 billion for Canada and $1.3 billion for Quebec. The study makes the important point that, given the reduction in the rate of increase of established programs financing, after seven or eight years cash transfers to Quebec will first disappear and then turn negative. But the reduction in transfers will reduce the federal share of funding of health and post-secondary education to 37 percent in 1990-91 from 47.9 percent in 1977-78 while maintaining constraints on provincial management of these programs.

Next, the Quebec Ministry of Finance describes the workings of the equalization formula, which raises the fiscal capacity of provinces up towards the level of the five provinces making up the standard (Quebec, Ontario, Manitoba, Saskatchewan, and British Columbia). In 1989-90 Quebec's equalization entitlements were $3.6 billion out of a total of $7.8 billion, which represents $533 per capita in Quebec compared to an average of $705 for recipient provinces. Unfortunately, the ministry argues, a ceiling limiting the increase of equalization to the cumulative growth of GNP will result in a $1,238 million reduction in total equalization in 1990-91, out of which Quebec will lose $749 million. They also note that, even after equalization, a gap of 13.8 percent in fiscal capacity exists and will be increased to 15.7 percent by the ceiling.

The ministry argues that federal transfer programs increasingly favour the better off provinces. As evidence, the ministry cites the fact that from 1984 to 1988 transfers grew at an annual average rate of 7.7 percent for non-equalization receiving provinces compared to 5.7 percent for equalization receiving provinces (and 8.1 percent for Ontario versus 3.5 percent for Quebec). This is attributed to four factors:

1) Cost sharing favours provinces which have a greater capacity to spend.

2) The cuts in established programs financing have been made on an equal per capita basis.

3) The less well-off provinces have had to increase their tax rates more than the other provinces.

4) Once the equalization ceiling was reached, the equalization receiving provinces have not received equalization for the tax increases.

The ministry neglects to acknowledge that the federal government has made some efforts to accommodate the less well-off provinces by applying the 5 per-cent limit only for increases in Canada Assistance Plan payments to non-equalization receiving provinces. Also, it is worth noting that restraining the increase in equalization to the growth of GNP cannot be considered severe restraint. Equalization would have grown more rapidly than GNP because of tax increases in the five provinces included in the standard, particularly Ontario. The slow growth of equalization in Quebec over the period stemmed in part from the end in 1985-86 of transitional payments which had been introduced to smooth the move to the 1982 equalization formula. Thus, the growth of equalization during this period does not reflect the longer run growth which would be generated by the formula. In my view, the ministry overstates its case, but still makes some valid points.

The ministry concludes that transfer programs need to be reviewed to improve redistribution and to stop impeding provinces' efforts to manage their expenditures through shared cost programs and standards. This is a federalist conclusion—in no way can it be interpreted as sovereigntist. Almost any other equalization receiving province might make the same argument.

Study 9

" A *Pro Forma* Analysis of Public Finances Under the Hypothesis of Quebec Sovereignty," by the Secretariat
                                                    (Commission, 1991b, pp.393-562)

This study, which was prepared by the secretariat of the commission, carries out a *pro forma* analysis of the public finances of a sovereign Quebec using 1990-91 as the reference year. *Pro forma* analysis is a technique used by accountants to prepare estimates of the financial statements of enterprises' performance under certain hypothetical as-

sumptions. It is usually, as it is in this study, complemented by sensitivity analysis involving a base case and alternative scenarios.

The secretariat assumes that all of the revenues currently raised by
the federal government in Quebec would become revenues of the
Quebec government and that all expenditures made by the federal
government in Quebec would be assumed by the Quebec government.
The analysis clearly distinguishes the impact of the sharing of assets and
liabilities. The secretariat acknowledges the obvious: there would have
to be negotiations to settle this question, and it is impossible to know in
advance their result.

Pro forma balance sheet of the federal government

The secretariat proposes a method to construct a *pro forma* balance
of the federal government for the purpose of the succession of states and
for the provision of order of magnitude estimates of the elements in this
balance. Pension liabilities and all other assets and liabilities are treated
separately. The main source of data used is the Public Accounts of
Canada, which is supplemented with data from Statistics Canada's
National Balance Sheet, the Study on the Financial Reporting of Federal
Government carried out by the U.S. General Accounting Office and the
Auditor General, the Nielsen Report, and an exploratory study carried
out for the commission by the accounting firm, Raymond, Chabot,
Martin, Paré & Cie.

Table 8 shows the balance sheet prepared by the secretariat for the
federal government's non-pension assets and liabilities. It is consolidated with the Bank of Canada's balance sheet. A few explanatory
comments might be useful. The stars (*) indicate the categories of
financial assets for which the secretariat has adjusted the Public Accounts data because of additional information. The $72 billion estimate
for the value of non-financial assets is based on the Nielsen Report's $50
billion estimate for 1984 and then scaled up to reflect the growth in the
federal government's capital stock to 1990. The accumulated deficit
reflects the difference between assets and liabilities. Pension liabilities,
which are not included in the table, amounted to $70,997 million as of
March 31, 1990.

TABLE 8

PRO FORMA **BALANCE SHEET OF THE FEDERAL
GOVERNMENT FOR THE PURPOSE OF SUCCESSION
OF STATES AS OF MARCH 31, 1990**
(Millions of Dollars)

ASSETS		LIABILITIES	
FINANCIAL ASSETS*	57,195	1) Currency in circulation	19,404
1) Exchange Fund and Foreign Currency Accounts*	21,228	2) Bank deposits	3,082
2) Loans, investments and advances and surplus of crown corporations*	26,312	3) Unmatured debt held outside of government accounts (excluding the Bank of Canada)	272,976
3) Accounts receivable*	5,993	-Treasury bills	106,890
		-Marketable bonds	121,659
4) Funds in transit	2,136	-Non-marketable bonds	42,804
		-Canada bills	1,446
5) Other assets	1,526	-Notes and loans	177
		4) Other Liabilities	34,127
NON-FINANCIAL ASSETS*	72,000		
TOTAL ASSETS	129,195		
ACCUMULATED DEFICIT**	200,394		
TOTAL OF ASSETS AND ACCUMULATED DEFICIT	329,589	TOTAL LIABILITIES	329,589

* Adjusted amounts.
** Accumulated deficit equals liabilities minus financial and non-financial assets. It is a concept taken from "A Study on Federal Government Financial Reporting," a joint study of the Office of the Auditor General of Canada and the United States General Accounting Office, March 1986.
Source: Commission sur l'avenir politique et constitutionnel du Québec (1991b, p.415).

Quebec's share of the federal balance sheet

The secretariat's proposed methodology for sharing assets and liabilities is based on the principle that part of the debt Quebec assumes should be based on its share of total federal assets. But one of the "assets" considered is the accumulated deficit, which is not really an asset. Furthermore, since the debt was not incurred to purchase assets, there is no reason why the debt split should be based on asset shares.

For financial assets, the secretariat lists the assets that Quebec would share either totally or as a minority shareholder. One criterion used is to select crown corporations which do business almost exclusively in Quebec. Another is to select corporations in which it would be useful for Quebec to retain a minority ownership. These criteria of picking and choosing result in the extremely low 3.8 percent share of financial assets as shown in table 9, which depresses Quebec's share of assets.

With respect to federal non-financial assets, the secretariat assumes that Quebec's share would be equivalent to the ratio between the value of these assets situated in Quebec and the total value of the assets located in Canada and elsewhere in the world. Since estimates of the geographic distribution of the value of these assets were not available, data from the Canadian Tax Foundation on the distribution of transfers to municipalities in lieu of taxes were used to estimate that $13 billion or 18 percent of federal non-financial assets were located in Quebec (table 9).

For the accumulated deficit, which again is not really an asset, the secretariat argues that it represents future tax liabilities and consequently should be shared based on Quebec's portion of total federal taxes, which is much less than Quebec's share of population. The secretariat argues that this criterion would be applied if Quebec were to remain in Confederation and that the criterion should not be changed if Quebec were to decide to leave. The secretariat is essentially arguing that Quebec should be able to enjoy the benefits of membership in the Canadian federation even if it leaves.

Another equally plausible interpretation of the accumulated deficit or indeed the net debt would be that it represents past deficits, which the secretariat's analysis in study 7 suggests were disproportionately higher in Quebec. These deficits could be considered net benefits purchased on credit which Quebec derived from Confederation. If Quebec were to decide to leave, it should pay back these benefits, resulting in a much higher than per capita share of federal assets. The cumulative net lending from the federal government in Quebec (the Provincial Economic Accounts equivalent of the federal deficit in Quebec) from 1961 to 1989 was equal to 30.9 percent of the total compared to a population share of 25.4 percent.[1]

The specific quantitative estimate prepared by the secretariat is based on the Provincial Economic Accounts data on the provincial distribution of tax revenues. Inconsistent with the analysis in the secretariat's study 7 and the analysis later in this study, no adjustment is made to the data to distribute certain indirect tax revenue based on consumption instead of production. In calculating Quebec's share, the period after the 1972 tax reform is used. The final figure after an adjustment for the special Quebec abatements is 22.8 percent (table 9). The secretariat estimates that, by adding up the shares of the three components of assets, Quebec's share of total assets would be 18.5 percent.

To estimate Quebec's share of liabilities if there were no formal monetary union between Quebec and Canada, the secretariat assumes that Quebec would still use the Canadian dollar as legal tender. The secretariat argues that in this case, where there would be no formal sharing of Bank of Canada profits, the division of the debt should exclude that part of the debt held by the Bank of Canada. The secretariat thus applies its estimated 18.5 percent share of assets to the federal non-pension fund liabilities net of debt held by the Bank of Canada to yield an estimate of Quebec's share of non-pension fund liabilities (table 10). According to the secretariat, the government of Quebec would have to assume the interest only on the debt. The debt itself would remain an obligation of the federal government, and Quebec would only assume the obligations based on a schedule to be negotiated.

Quebec's share of pension fund liabilities was calculated by the secretariat based on the proportion of federal employees working in Quebec. The share was estimated separately for each federal pension fund; the total share amounts to 13.3 percent. This low pension share pulls down the Quebec share of total financial liabilities, including pension funds, to 17.5 percent. In my view, the pension liabilities of the federal government represent payments for past consumption of government services provided by public servants. As such, there is no reason why they should be treated any differently than other government liabilities. The location of the public servants entitled to the pensions should be irrelevant.

TABLE 9

QUEBEC'S SHARE OF TOTAL FEDERAL GOVERNMENT ASSETS AS OF MARCH 31, 1990
(Millions of Dollars)

BASE SCENARIO A	Value of Assets in the Balance Sheet of Succession**	*Share of Quebec*	
		% of Assets	Amount
FINANCIAL ASSETS	57,195	3.8*	2,169
1) Exchange operations accounts and deposits in foreign currencies	21,228	0.0	
2) Loans, investments and advances and surpluses of crown corporations	26,312	8.2*	2,169
3) Accounts receivable	5,993	0.0	
4) Funds in transit	2,136	0.0	
5) Other financial assets	1,526	0.0	
NON-FINANCIAL ASSETS	72,000	18.0	12,960
TOTAL ASSETS	129,195	11.7*	15,129
ACCUMULATED DEFICIT	200,394	22.8	45,690
TOTAL	329,589	18.5*	60,819

*Percentage deducted from the amounts.
** See table 8.
Source: Commission sur l'avenir politique et constitutionnel du Québec (1991b, p.427).

The impact of the secretariat's proposed sharing of assets and liabilities on revenues and expenditures is provided in table 11. The additional revenue of $40 million is relatively small because of the particular financial assets selected. The increase in public debt charges of $7.1 billion would have a major impact on the budgetary position of the Quebec government.

In my view, the methodology proposed by the secretariat is arbitrary: it results in an unacceptably low 17.5 percent share of federal liabilities for Quebec. A fairer approach would be to agree to a global share based on population. All assets and liabilities would have to be evaluated. The specific assets or shares of specific assets taken by each party would then have to be negotiated. The value of the specific asset transfers should be tallied up and the appropriate amount of liabilities, which would be necessary to equalize the per capita value of liabilities net of assets of each party, would have to be transferred as a final settlement. This method would have the advantage of not being based on the existing arbitrary geographic distribution of assets.

TABLE 10

QUEBEC'S SHARE IN THE LIABILITIES OF THE FEDERAL GOVERNMENT AS OF MARCH 31, 1990
(Millions of Dollars)

BASE SCENARIO (A)	*Liabilities in the Balance Sheet of Succession**	*Share of Quebec*	
		% of Liabilities	*Amount*
MONETARY LIABILITIES			
- Currency in circulation	19,404	Variations in Quebec's Share would be determined by the balance of payments of Quebec	
- Bank deposits	3,082		
Total Monetary Liabilities	24,486		
FINANCIAL LIABILITIES			
- Unmatured Debt outstanding (excluding holdings of the Bank of Canada)	272,976	18.5	50,500
- Other liabilities	34,127	18.5	6,314
Total Financial Liabilities	307,103	18.5	56,814

Source: Commission sur l'avenir politique et constitutionnel du Québec (1991b, p.431).

TABLE 11

IMPACTS OF SHARING THE BALANCE SHEET OF SUCCESSION ON THE BALANCE SHEET, REVENUES AND EXPENDITURES OF THE GOVERNMENT OF QUEBEC (Millions of Dollars)

BASE SCENARIO A

	Impact on the balance sheet of Quebec	Impact on budgetary revenues	Impact on budgetary expenditures
SHARING OF ASSETS			
- Financial assets	2,169	40	-
- Non-financial assets	12,960	____	Imputed to the operating expenditures of departments
	15,129	40	
SHARING OF LIABILITIES			Debt service
- Unmatured debt outstanding (excluding (excluding holdings of the Bank of Canada)	50,500		6,022
- Other Liabilities	6,314		144
- Pension funds	9,456		939
Total	66,270		7,104

Source: Commission sur l'avenir politique et constitutionnel du Québec (1991b, p.435.

The estimation of Quebec's share of federal revenues and expenditures before the division of assets and liabilities

The secretariat calculated Quebec's share of federal revenues by applying the Quebec share of revenues in 1989 from the Provincial Economic Accounts to federal revenues from the Public Accounts for 1990-91. Using the interprovincial distribution of consumer expenditures and the tax base of the Goods and Services Tax, an adjustment was made to distribute certain indirect taxes based on consumption rather than production. The result was an estimated $24,461 million increase in Quebec revenues, amounting to 20.3 percent of total federal government budgetary revenues.

In estimating Quebec's share of expenditures, the secretariat distinguished three categories:

1) the public debt charges which was distributed based on Quebec's assumed share of the debt;

2) federal transfers to the provinces, which would not be an expenditure for Quebec, but a lost revenue;

3) other federal expenditures.

The secretariat allocated other federal expenditures based on an assessment of how much of a given program provided services to Quebeckers, on indicators such as the distribution of population or GDP where no information was available, and on the expenditures of other ministries and agencies attributable to Quebec for central agencies.

By adding up of Quebec's share of spending of all the ministries and agencies, the secretariat estimates that Quebec would have to assume $18,163 million in additional expenditures or 22 percent of total federal expenditures. This estimate does not include the additional public debt charges resulting from the division of assets and liabilities.

The secretariat considered two scenarios. In scenario one no cost savings from rationalization were assumed. In scenario two, based on estimates of Quebec and federal costs per employee or taxpayer in transport, communication and revenue collection, the secretariat calculated that $522 million could be saved.

Table 13 provides the *pro forma* summary financial statement of Quebec which incorporate the estimates of increases in revenues and expenditures but exclude any increase in public debt charges resulting from the distribution of assets and liabilities under both scenarios. The secretariat estimates the Quebec budgetary deficit would be increased by $499 million under scenario one and only $23 million under scenario two, for an average increase of $238 million. Using the Provincial Economic Accounts which suggested that the federal government's adjusted net balance in Quebec would be a net fiscal gain of $2.7 billion, it is difficult to reconcile these small increases with the secretariat's own analysis for 1988. It would appear that there are some federal expenditures revenues affecting Quebec which are not being taken properly into account in the secretariat's estimate of the increase in the budgetary deficit.

TABLE 12

PRO FORMA BUDGET OF THE GOVERNMENT OF QUEBEC
BUDGETARY BALANCE BEFORE SHARING THE BALANCE
SHEET OF SUCCESSION 1990-91 FISCAL YEAR
(Millions of Dollars)

	Expenditure Scenarios		
	I	II	*Average*
BUDGETARY REVENUES			
Actual Budgetary Revenues	33,571	33,571	33,571
Less: Revenues transferred from the Federal Government	6,797	6,797	6,797
Plus: Revenues recovered	24,461	24,461	24,461
PRO FORMA TOTAL REVENUES	51,235	51,235	51,235
BUDGETARY EXPENDITURES			
Actual Budgetary Expenditures	35,551	35,551	35,551
Plus: Additional Expenditures	18,163	17,641	17,902
PRO FORMA TOTAL EXPENDITURES	53,714	53,192	53,453
BUDGETARY BALANCE			
Actual Budgetary Balance	-1,980	-1,980	-1,980
Impact on Budgetary Balance before sharing the Balance Sheet of Succession	-499	+23	-238
PRO FORMA BUDGETARY BALANCE BEFORE SHARING THE BALANCE SHEET OF SUCCESSION	-2,479	-1,957	-2,218

Source: Commission sur l'avenir politique et constitutionnel du Québec (1991b, p.471).

Quebec's pro forma financial operations after sharing assets and liabilities

The secretariat estimates that, after taking into account the increase in public debt charges of $7,064 million, Quebec's budgetary deficit would increase from $2,218 million to $9,282 million. Financial requirements would increase by only $6,480 to $7,455 million because there would be a $822 million non-budgetary source of funds from Quebec's additional expenditures to public sector pensions.

To estimate Quebec's budgetary position, the secretariat assumes that 19.5 percent of liabilities are assumed by Quebec (scenario B), or that 17 percent of liabilities are assumed by Quebec (scenario C), or, in the base case, that 18.5 percent are assumed by Quebec (scenario A). This relatively minor range of variation in assumptions never approaches the population share of 25.4 percent—a reasonable, if not the most reasonable, alternative. In my view, ignoring the more difficult scenarios makes the secretariat's sensitivity analysis highly misleading: it gives Quebeckers a falsely rosy picture of what a sovereign Quebec may face. Nevertheless, the secretariat's estimates are presented in table 13.

The secretariat provides its estimates of the deficit and debt of both Quebec and Canada if Quebec were to become sovereign (table 14). The Quebec deficit would increase from 1.2 percent to 5.8 percent of GDP. Quebec debt as a percentage of GDP would increase from 26.4 percent to 63.9 percent.

In spite of the important share of the public debt assumed by Quebec, the secretariat argues Quebec's financial position would be better than Canada's. Quebec's debt to GDP ratio would only be 63.9 percent, compared to 72.1 percent for Canada. This surprising result merits some explanation. The secretariat notes that Canada would keep a proportionally larger part of the federal government's assets and hence a larger part of the debt. This is, of course, true. Assets are so much smaller than debt that a proportionally larger share of both adds up to an increase in the debt burden. In effect, the secretariat is proposing to leave Canada with a disproportionate share of the debt burden. It is no wonder that the financial position of Quebec improves and Canada deteriorates. Because the province of Quebec already has a much higher debt ratio than the other provinces (26.4 percent of GDP compared to 13.7 percent of GDP, according to the secretariat's figures), the increase in the debt ratio for Canada, including the nine provinces, is less than half of that for the federal government (table 14). The separation of Quebec would lower the average debt ratio of provincial governments by three percentage points.

TABLE 13

PRO FORMA BUDGETARY DEFICIT AND NET FINANCIAL REQUIREMENTS OF THE GOVERNMENT OF QUEBEC FOR 1990-91 FOR THREE SCENARIOS FOR THE SHARING OF THE BALANCE SHEET OF SUCCESSION
(Millions of Dollars)

	Base Scenario A	Scenario B	Scenario C
PRO FORMA BUDGETARY DEFICIT			
- Millions of dollars	-9,282	-9,615	-8,783
- Percentage of GDP	5.8	6.0	5.5
PRO FORMA NET FINANCIAL REQUIREMENTS			
- Millions of dollars	-7,455	-7,788	-6,955
- Percentage of GDP	4.7	4.9	4.4

Source: Commission sur l'avenir politique et constitutionnel du Québec (1991b, p.481).

On the basis of these artificially low estimates of the debt burden of a sovereign Quebec, the secretariat claims that the Quebec debt would be between 53 and 58 percent of GDP (56 percent for scenario A). Based on the OECD's definition, these estimates exclude debt to pension funds, so that the Quebec debt would be comparable to small countries' average debt of 55.6 percent and to European countries' debt of 57.4 percent (figure 2). This estimate is particularly surprising since the secretariat's estimates of gross debt for both Quebec and Canada (56 and 65.6 percent respectively) are well below the OECD's estimate of 71.0 percent for Canada's gross debt. Furthermore, the estimate of 71.0 percent is provided in the same OECD table from which the secretariat takes its estimates of other OECD countries' debt. Evidently, the secretariat has omitted some component of debt for Quebec and Canada in its comparisons. The most likely candidate for exclusion is municipal debt, but they could have also inappropriately accounted for pension liabilities. The secretariat's international comparisons demonstrate only that it would be possible for Quebec to maintain an average debt level if Quebec were not to assume its fair share of the federal debt and not to count all of its existing debt.

TABLE 14

FINANCIAL INDICATORS FOR THE BASE SCENARIO A, 1990-91

| | Quebec | | Canada[3] | | Federal Government | |
	Actual	Scenario	Actual	Scenario	Actual	Scenario
DEFICIT[1]						
- Millions of dollars	-1,980	9,282	-37,323	-28,041	-30,500	-23,198
- Percentage of GDP	1.2	5.8	5.5	5.4	4.5	4.4
DEBT[2]						
- Percentage of GDP	26.4	63.9	70.2	72.1	53.5	58.4
DEBT SERVICE[1]						
- Percentage of GDP	2.8	7.2	8.2	8.4	6.3	6.8
- Percentage of budgetary revenues	13.2	22.5	22.7	23.6	35.6	37.2

[1] In 1990-91.

[2] Debt as of March 31, 1990: Unmatured debt and pension fund accounts.

[3] Actual for Canada: the federal government and the ten provinces.
Scenario A: the federal government and the nine provinces.

Note: It is not correct to compare financial indicators for Quebec under one of the scenarios for the succession of states with the federal government either in the actual situation or in case of one of the scenarios. Comparisons should be made between two governments exercising the same jurisdictions.

Source: Commission sur l'avenir politique et constitutionnel du Québec (1991b, p.484).

FIGURE 2

INTERNATIONAL COMPARISON OF GROSS PUBLIC DEBT/GDP (%), 1990

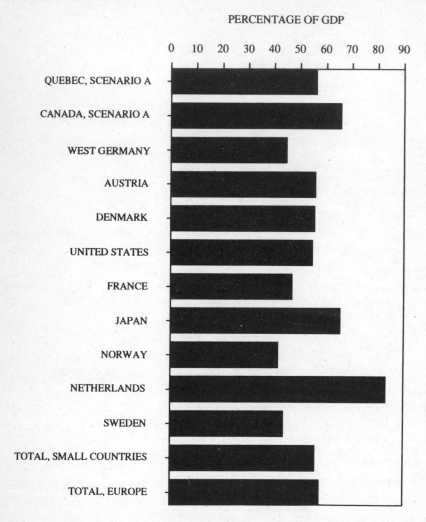

This is based on OECD data for national accounts gross financial liabilities less pension funds.

Source: Commission sur l'avenir politique et constitutionnel du Quebec (1991b, p. 489).

Conclusion

Without sharing assets and liabilities, the secretariat concludes, the impact of sovereignty on the public finances of Quebec would be small, increasing the budgetary deficit by only $200 million. In my view, such a small increase is surprising and difficult to square with the secretariat's own estimate of the federal government's adjusted net balance in Quebec.

The secretariat does emphasize that Quebec would inherit a constraining structure of expenditures. Of the $18 billion in additional expenditures, two-thirds would be made up of transfers to individuals, businesses, and local administrations, and one-third would be operating expenditures. But the secretariat does not believe that this would hinder the rationalization of spending.

Sharing assets and liabilities obviously has fundamental implications for the Quebec government's financial position. The secretariat stresses that it must be recognized that Quebeckers are already supporting the federal debt and interest payments through their contributions to federal revenues so that, if after sovereignty they continue to pay a similar share, their level of debt will not change. But this of course depends on what share of the debt they assume. If they assume their per capita share of the debt, their level of debt in relation to GDP would increase, and so would their public debt charges.

According to the secretariat, the method it proposed to share assets and liabilities was judged to be consistent with international law according to the opinion of two judicial experts. But the secretariat neglects to mention that almost anything which would be agreed to by Quebec and Canada would be consistent with international law. Naturally, therefore, the two experts were not able to rule out the secretariat's proposal. In fact, international law offers no firm guidance on the most appropriate split of assets and liabilities. The Vienna Convention on the Succession of States in Respect of State Property, Archives and Debt, 1983. has not been ratified by the major industrialized countries. Moreover, its application to a new state created from an existing state requires that the creation of the new state conform to the principles of the Charter of the United Nations, which demands the consent of the dismembered state. Also. debts to private creditors are not even covered by the Vienna convention. There is no one legally sanctioned method of dividing assets and liabilities under international law. Everything would be up for grabs at the negotiating table. The secretariat is misleading Quebeckers by implying that its proposal has special merit because it is consistent with international law.

Using the secretariat's methodology, the liabilities assumed by the Government of Quebec would be directly proportional to Quebec's share of assets. The division of pension liabilities would be proportional to the share of federal employees working in Quebec and participating in the pension plan. This would amount to $9.5 billion, or 13.3 percent of the total federal pension liabilities of $71 billion. Since it was not possible to establish precisely the share of the federal government's non-financial assets (estimated to be $72 billion in Quebec), three scenarios with different shares were used to establish Quebec's share of federal government liabilities at 18.5 percent, 19.5 percent, and 17 percent respectively in scenarios A, B, and C.

In all of the scenarios, Quebec's share of federal debt would be less than its share of GDP. Thus the debt to GDP ratios of Quebec would be less than that of the federal government and the nine other provinces taken together. The ratio of assets would also be less given the method of division proposed. Quebec's ratio of debt to GDP would be comparable to that of most other industrialized countries of similar size. These results, of course, depend critically on the method chosen. If a per capita criterion were used, which would be fair, the debt ratios would be higher than the rest of Canada's and higher than most industrialized countries'. It all depends on your point of view. The secretariat's estimates and conclusions need to be seen for what they are and taken with a large grain of salt. Masquerading as objective analysis, they are really nothing more than exercises in numerology designed to assuage the legitimate concerns of Quebeckers about the economic impacts of sovereignty.

Notes

1. Paul Boothe and Richard Harris (1991,p.2) have independently proposed the similar alternative of basing the distribution on historical benefits from the net federal spending by province as measured by Mansell and Schlenker (1990).

Chapter 4

The economic viability of a sovereign Quebec

Introduction

THIS CHAPTER CONSIDERS THE economic viability of a sovereign Quebec using something like the methodology which would be applied by the World Bank or a credit rating agency evaluating sovereign risk. Since Quebec is not a sovereign country and all the required data do not exist, it is not possible to carry out detailed assessments of performance, prospects, and the adequacy of current policies. But it is possible to assess the recent performance of the Quebec economy and its likely prospects if it continues as a province of Canada. It is also possible to adjust existing data to provide an estimate of fiscal and trade balances and of public and external debt of a sovereign Quebec. These estimates give an idea of the magnitude of any disequilibria that are likely to emerge and the related financing problems that may arise. Focusing on these disequilibria and the structural adjustment policies necessary to resolve them is the essence of the World Bank approach.

The second section of this chapter examines the recent performance of the Quebec economy and its prospects. The third considers the prospects for Quebec's longer-term population growth. The fourth section reviews Quebec's industrial structure and interregional trade links. The fifth section looks at the trade sector and current account balance and related external debt. The sixth section compares the Quebec economy to that of the rest of Canada. The seventh section provides an international comparative perspective for the Quebec economy. The eighth section looks at fiscal deficits and debt and presents some estimates of deficits and debt for a sovereign Quebec. The ninth section provides a comparison of Quebec's fiscal position and capacity with other provinces. The tenth section discusses the impact of uncertainty over sovereignty on the borrowing costs of the Quebec government. The eleventh section offers an overall assessment on the viability of a sovereign Quebec.

Recent performance and prospects of the Quebec economy

Performance

The Quebec economy grew strongly in 1987 and 1988, slowed in 1989, and turned down in 1990 (table 15). From 1987 to 1990, real growth in Quebec has been the same as in the rest of Canada, averaging about 3 percent. The growth has been slightly higher in Real Domestic Product per capita in Quebec where population growth has been slower. Business fixed investment has been the leading sector. Hydro-Quebec and the aluminum industry have been the biggest investors. At 9.3 percent in 1989, the unemployment rate was down substantially from its 1983 annual high of nearly 14 percent.

The strength of the Quebec economy was reflected in a greater degree of confidence among business leaders and citizens in the viability of the Quebec economy. This confidence was reinforced by the Canada-U.S. Free Trade Agreement which was perceived as lessening the dependence of the Quebec economy on trade with the rest of Canada.

The relative strength of Quebec's investment spending has contributed to the growing confidence of sovereigntists. Table 16 shows the industrial composition of the increased investment. Within manufacturing, a sector which exhibited solid growth, particularly over the last five

TABLE 15

RECENT ECONOMIC PERFORMANCE IN QUEBEC
(Percent Change)

	1987	*1988*	*1989*	*1990*
Real Demand				
Consumer expenditures	3.9	3.7	3.1	0.9
Bus. fixed investment	16.5	12.4	10.4	0.1
Residential construction	16.9	-1.3	-8.2	-1.6
Government expenditures	1.3	3.2	2.0	3.1
Final domestic demand	5.4	4.1	2.9	1.2
Gross domestic product	4.8	4.5	2.5	0.9
Other Indicators				
Housing starts (000)	73	59	49	47
Consumer price index	4.4	3.7	4.2	4.3
Employment	3.3	2.8	1.0	0.8
Unemployment rate (%)	10.3	9.4	9.3	10.1

Source: Statistics Canada except for 1990 real demand which is a forecast from Caisse de dépôt (1991, p.29).

years, the increase has been fairly narrowly based. Four industries—primary metals (primarily aluminum), paper and allied products, chemical and chemical products, and transportation equipment—account for 75 percent of the increase in investment. Primary metals and paper and allied products alone account for 58 percent of the increase. Outside of manufacturing, the increase has been more broadly based, with communications, trade, and financial and commercial services accounting for large shares of the increase. Investment in financial services was particulary strong. Miscellaneous utilities, which includes electrical utilities, has recorded substantial increases in investment spending. While it has picked up over the last five years, its growth has been relatively slow during the past decade. The pattern of spending on the James Bay hydroelectric development has been a determining factor behind the growth in this series. The relatively narrow base of Quebec's investment growth suggests that the growing confidence of sovereigntists in Quebec's economic future is not very solidly based.

TABLE 16

CAPITAL AND REPAIR EXPENDITURES IN QUEBEC
(Millions of Dollars)

	1980	1985	1990	Change in Investment			Average Growth Rate		
				1980-1985	1985-1990	1980-1990	1980-1985	1985-1990	1980-1990
Primary Industries									
Agriculture	692	736	796	44	60	104	1.2	1.6	1.4
Forestry	107	69	94	-38	25	-13	-8.5	6.5	-1.3
Mines, Quar. and Oil	681	577	644	-104	67	-37	-3.3	2.2	-0.6
Construction	356	446	749	90	303	393	4.6	10.9	7.7
Subtotal	1836	1827	2283	-9	456	447	-0.1	4.6	2.2
Manufacturing									
Food and Beverage	315	355	444	40	89	129	2.4	4.6	3.5
Tobacco	30	64	X[a]	34	X	X	16.1	X	X
Rubber	52	83	115	32	32	64	10.0	6.8	8.4
Leather	7	6	7	-2	2	-0	-4.8	4.8	-0.1
Textiles	115	108	136	-7	28	21	-1.3	4.7	1.7
Knitting Mills	25	11	13	-14	2	-12	-15.1	2.9	-6.5
Clothing	21	22	27	1	5	5	0.7	4.0	2.3
Wood	109	151	149	42	-2	41	6.8	-0.2	3.2
Furniture and Fixtures	17	18	28	1	10	11	0.8	9.2	4.9
Paper and Allied	581	995	1669	414	674	1089	11.4	10.9	11.1
Printing and Publishing	53	72	87	20	15	34	6.5	3.7	5.1
Primary Metal	570	1217	2455	647	1238	1885	16.4	15.1	15.7
Metal Fabricating	113	115	118	2	3	5	0.4	0.4	0.4
Machinery	69	119	192	50	73	123	11.5	10.1	10.8
Transportation Equip.	154	188	530	35	342	377	4.2	23.0	13.2
Electrical Products	85	195	277	109	82	191	18.0	7.3	12.5
Non-metallic Minerals	130	121	270	-9	149	140	-1.4	17.4	7.6
Petroleum and Coal	171	137	243	-34	107	73	-4.4	12.3	3.6
Chemical and Chem. Prod	330	405	864	75	459	534	4.2	16.4	10.1

TABLE 16 *(continued)*

	1980	1985	1990	Change in Investment			Average Growth Rate		
				1980- 1985	1985- 1990	1980- 1990	1980- 1985	1985- 1990	1980- 1990
Misc. Manufacturing	40	55	X	16	X	X	6.8	X	X
Capital Charged to Op.	231	332	631	101	299	400	7.6	13.7	10.6
Subtotal	3217	4769	8363	1552	3594	5146	8.2	11.9	10.0
Utilities Transportation	1141	1494	1540	353	46	399	5.5	0.6	3.0
Communication	937	1089	2025	153	935	1088	3.1	13.2	8.0
Misc. Utilities	2837	2146	4118	-690	1971	1281	-5.4	13.9	3.8
Subtotal	4915	4730	7682	-185	2952	2767	-0.8	10.2	4.6
Trade, Fin. and Commercial									
Trade	348	541	865	193	325	518	9.2	9.9	9.5
Finance	362	1053	2623	691	1570	2261	23.8	20.0	21.9
Commercial Services	1110	1713	2711	602	998	1600	9.1	9.6	9.3
Subtotal	1820	3306	6199	1486	2892	4378	12.7	13.4	13.0

[a] This information is not available.

Source: Statistics Canada, *Private and Public Investment in Canada*, Catalogue 61-205. Data for 1990 are revised intentions not actuals.

Prospects

The Quebec economy is currently suffering from the same recession which hit Canada last spring. The downturn has been most severe in Ontario and, to a lesser extent, Quebec, where the country's manufacturing sector is concentrated. The Quebec 1991 budget forecast shown in table 17 called for a more than 1 percent decline in real output this year (Quebec, Ministry of Finance, Appendix D, p.18). The actual decline would have been greater except for the continuation of large investment projects in the aluminum industry. The current recession is likely to be much milder than the one in 1981-82. The recession in Quebec, as in the rest of Canada, was precipitated by increases in interest rates and in the Canadian dollar, with the resulting sharp decline in the interest-sensitive sectors of investment, housing, and consumer durables. It was exacerbated by the recession in the United States which lowered demand for exports. The introduction of the Goods and Services Tax in January and Quebec's use of the opportunity to piggyback and increase its own sales tax also depressed consumer spending. Exports were also weak as the economies of trading partners weakened. Demand for pulp and paper, which represents about one-fifth of Quebec exports, was particularly depressed. Employment is forecast to decrease this year and unemployment to rise to approximately 12.4 percent.

The Quebec budget forecasts that the Quebec economy will recover from 1992 to 1994 with growth averaging around 3.5 percent. This is slightly weaker than the growth of the total Canadian economy, which is forecast in the federal budget to be 3.5 percent in 1992 and to average 4 percent from 1993 to 1996 (Canada, Department of Finance, 1991a, p.51). The Quebec recovery will be fuelled by the same factors behind the Canadian upturn, namely a drop in interest rates and an increase in U.S. growth. Aided by Quebec government mortgage assistance as well as lower interest rates, residential construction should be the leading sector in 1992. Consumer expenditures, while hampered by the application of the Quebec sales tax to services in 1992, should also still strengthen. Exports are expected to rebound as the U.S. economy recovers. By 1993 business investment should pick up strongly, spurred by the reimbursement of sales tax on investment purchases. In spite of the recovery, unemployment is forecast to remain high, averaging more than 11 percent from 1992 to 1994. Quebec's predicted unemployment rate is significantly higher than the Canadian unemployment rate projected by the federal government.

Other forecasters, such as the Conference Board, have a similar view of Quebec's short-term prospects (Conference Board, 1991, pp.15-17). It must be emphasized that these forecasts were based on the assumption that Quebec would remain part of Canada and that the economic upheaval which would be associated with separation would be avoided. These forecasts indicate that Quebec is currently in a recession and that it will take some time before the economy fully recovers. Quebec is experiencing an extremely fragile economic climate which puts a premium on prudent economic policy. It is not the best time to be subjecting the Quebec economy to the shock of separating from

Canada. Nevertheless, the confidence of Quebeckers in the economic viability of a sovereign Quebec has evidently not yet been shaken by the downturn, as it was during the 1981-82 recession following the 1980 referendum.

TABLE 17

MEDIUM-TERM ECONOMIC OUTLOOK FOR QUEBEC
(Percent Change)

	1991	*1992-94*
PRODUCTION		
- Gross Domestic Product	2.9	7.5
- Real Domestic Product	-1.1	3.5
COMPONENTS OF DEMAND		
- Non-residential Investment	5.2	7.8
- Housing Starts (000)	41.4	45.2
- Retail Sales (adjusted for GST)	-1.1	6.5
COMPONENTS OF INCOME		
- Wages and Salaries	2.4	6.6
- Personal Income	4.8	6.3
- Corporate Profits	-19.0	22.7
LABOUR MARKET		
- Labour Force	0.1	1.7
- Employment	-2.5	2.5
- Unemployment Rate (%)	12.4	11.2

Source: Quebec, Ministry of Finance (1991, Appendix D, p.18).

Population growth

The population of Quebec is expected to grow more slowly than the rest of Canada even if Quebec remains part of Canada. The lower population growth caused concerns in Quebec about the declining demographic and economic importance of Quebec within Canada.

Long-term population projections for Quebec and Canada, prepared by Tom McCormack of Strategic Projections Inc., an economic consulting firm specializing in demographics, are displayed in table 18. The projections reflect the current age and sex structure of the population and use age and sex specific mortality and fertility rates. International immigration is based on the federal government's announced 250,000 annual target. The slower growth of the Quebec population is evident in the decline in the share of total Canadian population from 25.3 percent in 1991 to 23.2 percent in 2011. The lower population growth for Quebec stems from the lower birth rate of Quebec women, the lower rate of international immigration to Quebec, and net emigration to the rest of Canada. The proportion of the Quebec population over 65 years old is expected to increase by four percentage points. Quebec will have to increase its spending on health and pensions relative to the rest of Canada.[1] The aging and relative decline in Quebec's population is expected to continue after 2011, when the leading edge of the baby boom population begins to reach retirement age.

The population projection considered assumes that Quebec will remain part of Canada. If Quebec were to become sovereign, there could be even less international immigration to Quebec and greater movement to the rest of Canada, especially among anglophones. A Centre de Recherche sur l'Opinion Publique (CROP) poll conducted in April indicated that 44 percent of English-speaking Quebeckers would not continue to live in an independent Quebec (Fontaine, 1991, p.A1). This would be an acceleration of the outflow identified in a recent study by SECOR Consultants which estimated that more than two hundred thousand anglophones have left Quebec during the last 15 years, since the Parti Québécois first came to power in 1976 (Picard, 1991). The decline in Quebec's demographic weight would be accentuated by an accession to sovereignty, making it more difficult to finance government spending and service the increased public debt of a sovereign Quebec.

Industrial structure and interregional trade links

A critical factor in determining the economic viability of a sovereign Quebec is its industrial structure and trade links.[2] The destination of Quebec shipments of manufacturers in 1984 is provided in table 19.

TABLE 18

POPULATION PROJECTIONS FOR CANADA AND QUEBEC
(Thousands)

	1991	2001	2011
Canada			
Population	26,932	29,981	32,431
International			
-Immigration	220	250	250
-Emigration	40	59	59
Population over 65 (%)	11.7	12.7	14.3
Quebec			
Population	6,818	7,261	7,509
Population Quebec/Canada (%)	25.3	24.2	23.2
International			
-Immigration	41	46	46
-Emigration	2	3	3
Net Interprovincial Immigration	-13	-13	-13
Population over 65 (%)	11.2	12.8	15.1

Source: Projections provided by Tom McCormack,
Strategic Projections Inc (May 1991).

Industries where interregional shipments account for a large proportion of total shipments (more than 40 percent) are tobacco products, rubber products, leather and allied products, textile products, clothing, and chemical and chemical products. Of these, textile products and clothing are the most important as measured by the value of interregional shipments. Foreign shipments are particularly important relative to the total for paper and allied products, primary metals, and transportation equipment. These shipments comprise Quebec's most important exporting manufacturing industries. In the aggregate, foreign shipments account for a lower proportion of total shipments than interregional shipments (21.3 percent compared to 26.5 percent).

Tables 20 and 21 provide information on the destination of manufacturer's shipments for the rest of Canada and for Ontario compared to Quebec. The relatively low proportion of manufacturer's shipments going from the rest of Canada or Ontario to Quebec, except in tobacco products and primary textiles, is noteworthy. The larger proportion of foreign shipments is also significant. Industries with a particularly high degree of foreign shipments are rubber products, wood, paper and allied products, machinery, transportation equipment, and electrical and electronic products. The extent to which Ontario has come to depend on foreign exports of transportation equipment is striking —76 percent of shipments of transportation equipment are outside of Canada, and transportation equipment accounts for about 63 percent of Ontario's foreign shipments of manufacturers.

The industrial breakdown of the $3.3 billion interregional trade surplus of Quebec's manufacturing industries is shown in table 22. The large surpluses in textile products, clothing, paper and allied products, primary metals, refined petroleum and coal products are noteworthy. Given the closure of a refinery in the east end of Montreal, it is likely that more recent data than 1984 would no longer show a surplus for refined petroleum and coal products. The large deficits in food industries and transportation equipment are also worth noting.

The extent to which the total $3.3 billion trade surplus is accounted for by the surpluses in the five "soft" industries (leather and allied products, primary textiles, textile products, clothing, and furniture and fixtures) is striking. These industries are labour-intensive and subject to strong foreign competition. Textiles and clothing, which are the most important of these industries, are protected by high tariffs and Voluntary Export Restraints (VER) under the Multi-Fibre Agreement (MFA). Effective rates of protection for textiles average 16.6 percent and Most Favoured Nation customs tariffs for clothing are as high as 25 percent. Import penetration in the market for textiles and clothing has been limited to 30 to 33 percent and 80 percent of imports are subject to restraint. Under the 1986 change to the VER, growth in base levels in previously restrained items was limited to 2 percent from 1987 to 1991. Also, the base levels for the four major exporters—Hong Kong, South Korea, Taiwan, and China—were reduced by 0.2 percent (Canadian International Trade Tribunal, 1990). The restraints are a more important source of protection than the high tariffs. Murray Smith estimates that the combined tariff equivalent of the tariffs and the VER ranges from 30 to 70 percent (Smith, 1991, p.6).

TABLE 19

DESTINATION OF QUEBEC SHIPMENTS OF MANUFACTURERS, 1984

	Rest of Canada		Foreign	
	$ Million	% of Total	$ Million	% of Total
10 Food Ind.	1720	20.3	659	7.8
11 Beverage Ind.	227	19.3		
12 Tobacco Products	503	67.3		
15 Rubber Products	256	66.7		
16 Plastic Products	287	32.7		
17 Leather & Allied Prod.	193	43.7		
18 Primary Textile	517	33.7		
19 Textile Products	624	51.7		
24 Clothing	1445	45.7		
25 Wood	342	14.3	487	20.4
26 Furniture & Fixtures	340	37.6		
27 Paper & Allied Prod.	1260	21.5	2883	49.2
28 Printing, Publish. & Allied	587	23.5		
29 Primary Metal	1222	26.1	2138	45.7
30 Fabricated Metal Products	695	21.5	860	26.6
31 Machinery	219	21.6	231	22.8
32 Transportation Equipment	692	16.1	2682	62.3
33 Electrical & Electronic Prod.	948	31.9	995	33.4
35 Non-metallic Mineral Prod.	144	12.8	120	10.7
36 Refined Petrol. & Coal Prod.	1371	26.6		
37 Chemical & Chemical Prod.	1579	44.5	320	9.0
39 Other Manufacturing	223	26.1		
ALL MANUFACTURING INDUSTRIES	15075	26.5	12132	21.3

Source: Statistics Canada, *Destinations of Shipments of Manufacturers 1984*, Catalogue 31-530, April 1988. Totals do not add because data is incomplete due to confidentiality.

TABLE 20

DESTINATION OF REST OF CANADA SHIPMENTS OF MANUFACTURERS, 1984

	Quebec		Foreign	
	$ Million	% of Total	$ Million	% of Total
10 Food Ind.	2152	9.3	1979	8.5
11 Beverage Ind.	93	2.8	483	14.3
12 Tobacco Products	233	27.7	0	0.0
15 Rubber Products	274	12.9	662	31.2
16 Plastic Products	237	9.0	317	12.0
17 Leather & Allied Prod.	142	17.1	0	0.0
18 Primary Textile	461	38.7	241	20.1
19 Textile Products	187	14.2	135	10.2
24 Clothing	304	15.1	152	7.6
25 Wood	272	3.6	3142	41.4
26 Furniture & Fixtures	163	7.7	316	14.9
27 Paper & Allied Prod.	784	6.8	6167	53.1
28 Printing, Publish. & Allied	245	4.0	145	2.3
29 Primary Metal	592	5.0	2882	24.5
30 Fabricated Metal Products	546	6.1	1003	11.2
31 Machinery	314	5.4	1805	30.9
32 Transportation Equipment	1118	3.3	24700	73.5
33 Electrical & Electronic Prod.	867	10.0	2662	30.8
35 Non-metallic Mineral Prod.	307	7.4	535	13.0
36 Refined Petrol. & Coal Prod.	586	3.2	1057	5.8
37 Chemical & Chemical Prod.	1532	11.2	1924	14.1
39 Other Manufacturing	334	8.7	624	16.3
ALL MANUFACTURING INDUSTRIES	11744	6.8	50310	29.1

Source: Statistics Canada, *Destinations of Shipments of Manufacturers 1984*, Catalogue 31-530, April 1988. Totals do not add because data is incomplete due to confidentiality.

TABLE 21

DESTINATION OF ONTARIO SHIPMENTS OF MANUFACTURERS, 1984

	Quebec		Foreign	
	$ Million	% of Total	$ Million	% of Total
10 Food Ind.	1502	12.1	525	4.2
11 Beverage Ind.	0	0.0	299	14.9
12 Tobacco Products	233	27.7	0	0.0
15 Rubber Products	0	0.0	220	14.9
16 Plastic Products	221	10.7	225	10.8
17 Leather & Allied Prod.	0	0.0	0	0.0
18 Primary Textile	436	41.0	152	14.3
19 Textile Products	174	15.6	89	8.0
24 Clothing	221	15.6	32	2.3
25 Wood	109	6.1	407	22.6
26 Furniture & Fixtures	154	8.7	237	13.4
27 Paper & Allied Prod.	665	11.4	1950	33.3
28 Printing, Publish. & Allied	236	5.4	59	1.3
29 Primary Metal	532	5.6	2174	23.0
30 Fabricated Metal Products	512	7.4	887	12.7
31 Machinery	302	7.1	1515	35.4
32 Transportation Equipment	934	3.0	23912	75.9
33 Electrical & Electronic Prod.	786	10.2	2329	30.3
35 Non-metallic Mineral Prod.	279	10.5	473	17.9
36 Refined Petrol. & Coal Prod.	0	0.0	857	9.7
37 Chemical & Chemical Prod.	1345	13.1	1083	10.6
39 Other Manufacturing	322	10.2	513	16.3
ALL MANUFACTURING INDUSTRIES	9701	8.0	38051	31.3

Source: Statistics Canada, *Destinations of Shipments of Manufacturers 1984*, Catalogue 31-530, April 1988. Totals do not add because data is incomplete due to confidentiality.

TABLE 22

INTERPROVINCIAL TRADE SURPLUS OF QUEBEC MANUFACTURING INDUSTRIES, 1984
(Millions of Dollars)

	Exports	Imports	Balance
10 Food Ind.	1720	2152	-431
11 Beverage Ind.	227	93	134
12 Tobacco Products	503	233	270
15 Rubber Products	256	274	-18
16 Plastic Products	287	237	50
17 Leather & Allied Prod.	193	142	51
18 Primary Textile	517	461	56
19 Textile Products	624	187	438
24 Clothing	1445	304	1141
25 Wood	342	272	70
26 Furniture & Fixtures	340	163	177
27 Paper & Allied Prod.	1260	784	475
28 Printing, Publish. & Allied	587	245	343
29 Primary Metal	1222	592	630
30 Fabricated Metal Products	695	546	149
31 Machinery	219	314	-95
32 Transportation Equipment	692	1118	-426
33 Electrical & Electronic Prod.	948	867	81
35 Non-metallic Mineral Prod.	144	307	-164
36 Refined Petrol. & Coal Prod.	1371	586	784
37 Chemical & Chemical Prod.	1579	1532	47
39 Other Manufacturing	223	334	-111
ALL MANUFACTURING INDUSTRIES	15075	11744	3331

Source: Statistics Canada, *Destinations of Shipments of Manufacturers 1984*, Catalogue 31-530, April 1988. These figures are not exact because Statistics Canada withholds some information on interregional shipments in order to preserve confidentiality.

TABLE 23

EMPLOYMENT AND VALUE ADDED IN SOFT INDUSTRIES IN QUEBEC, 1987

	Employment			Value Added		
Industry Group	Number	% of Total Manufact. in Quebec	% of Total Industry In Canada	$ Million	% of Total Manufact. in Quebec	% of Total Industry in Canada
Leather and Allied Products	8162	1.6	37.5	237	0.8	36.0
Primary Textiles	13976	2.7	53.9	610	2.0	42.1
Textile Products	16009	3.1	46.0	677	2.2	47.7
Clothing	65539	12.6	58.5	1891	6.2	55.9
Furniture and Fixtures	20446	3.9	33.2	695	2.3	31.3
TOTAL	124132	23.9	48.5	4111	13.6	45.0

Source: Statistics Canada, *Manufacturing Industries of Canada, National and Provincial Areas*, Catalogue 31–203, 1987.

Information on the structure of the "soft" industries in 1987 is provided in table 23. These industries employ over 124,000 people and account for about 24 percent of total manufacturing employment in Quebec. Their share of total value added is much less than their share of employment, only accounting for 13.5 percent of value added. These "soft" industries are concentrated geographically in Quebec—48.5 percent of employment and 45 percent of value added in these industries were located in Quebec.

Employment in the soft industries, particulary in textiles and clothing, has declined in the face of tough competition, going from 155,000 in 1974 to 124,000 in 1987. But the adjustment has been slowed by high tariffs and especially by quotas. Further adjustment will be required. In a sovereign Quebec, the soft industries would be highly vulnerable to changes in Canadian commercial policy. Moreover, changes are likely as Canadian consumers cannot be expected to bear the costs of protecting Quebec soft industries.

To assess the possible impacts of Quebec sovereignty, it would be useful to have current data on effective rates of protection by industry and on average effective rates for Quebec and the rest of Canada to assess the possible impacts of Quebec sovereignty. Unfortunately, such data are not publicly available.

External balance and debt

No good timely information has been published on Quebec's external balance or external debt. Data are available on manufacturer's shipments. In 1984, the latest year for which data are available, Quebec had a surplus in interregional trade of $3.3 billion or 3.3 percent of GDP with the rest of Canada. It was the only province other than Ontario to run a surplus. Data are also available on energy trade. In 1987, Quebec imported more than $2 billion in oil and around $700 million in natural gas, but it had net exports of hydroelectricity of about $600 million. Hydroelectricity is a definite strength of the Quebec economy. Finally, there are data on interregional trade in agriculture and mineral products. In 1984, Quebec had a deficit of $523 million in agriculture products and $2.7 billion in its trade in minerals with other provinces. The Statistics Canada provincial input-output model contains consistent information on Quebec's interprovincial and international trade balances covering all goods and services. It indicates that, in 1984, the most recent year available, Quebec had a deficit in its interprovincial trade of $1 billion and in international trade of $3.2 billion, for a total deficit of $4.2 billion or 4.2 percent of GDP (Proulx and Cauchy, 1991, pp.73-74).

The Provincial Economic Accounts provide relatively timely estimates by province of net exports, a key component of the current account balance. Unfortunately, since net exports are measured residually, the data also include a statistical discrepancy to make expenditures add up to income. This discrepancy makes the data somewhat suspect as an indicator of net exports. Nevertheless, since they are the only complete data which are available, they are shown in table 24. Canada ran a large surplus on net exports of $7.2 billion, or 1.1 percent of GDP in 1989. This surplus does not include the large deficit on interest and dividends which transforms it into a current account deficit of $16.6 billion, or 3 percent of GDP. Following a period of deficits, Quebec's surplus on net exports was so small in 1989 as to be in virtual balance. In contrast, Ontario ran a very large surplus of $15.5 billion, or 5.7 percent of GDP, following a string of similar surpluses. The rest of the country, including Ontario, has been running surpluses amounting to around 1.5 percent of GDP.

These piecemeal and somewhat unreliable data do not provide a definitive reading on Quebec's external balance. But they do suggest that Quebec's position is much weaker than Canada as a whole or the rest of Canada. A sovereign Quebec could therefore have trouble servicing its external debt if it did not take steps to strengthen its current account balance. A surplus of net exports on a GDP basis large enough to offset Quebec's deficit on interest and dividends would probably be in the neighbourhood of 2 to 3 percent of GDP. Given that in 1989 Quebec's net exports were in approximate balance, it would be necessary to transfer approximately 2 to 3 percent of its domestic consumption to net exports in order to produce a more sustainable current account balance.

TABLE 24

NET EXPORTS PLUS STATISTICAL DISCREPANCY
FROM THE PROVINCIAL ECONOMIC ACCOUNTS

	1986	*1987*	*1988*	*1989*
Canada				
-millions of dollars	3840	3639	8502	7215
-percent of GDP	0.8	0.7	1.4	1.1
Quebec				
-millions of dollars	-1396	-2358	858	151
-percent of GDP	-1.2	-1.8	0.6	0.1
Ontario				
-millions of dollars	11106	10170	14563	15496
-percent of GDP	5.5	4.5	5.8	5.7
Rest of Canada incl. Ontario				
-millions of dollars	5236	5997	7644	7064
-percent of GDP	1.4	1.4	1.7	1.4

Source: Statistics Canada, *Provincial Economic Accounts.*

In the absence of any data on Quebec, information on Canada's current account balance and external debt is presented in table 25. The large Canadian current account deficit is striking. At 2.6 percent of GDP in 1989, it is larger in relative terms than the current account balances of all the Group of Seven countries except for the United Kingdom. Even the much discussed current account deficit of the United States is not as large in relative terms. Many years of current account deficits have made Canada a large net debtor on the international investment account. In 1989, the most recent year for which data are available, net external debt was $229 billion, or 35 percent of GDP, or 141 percent of exports.

Canada is the industrialized world's second largest debtor behind the U.S., which had net external indebtedness of $658 million U.S. in 1989. Canada's debt 1989 was $194 billion in U.S. dollars, larger than that of the other biggest international debtors, including Brazil (U.S. $112.7 billion), Mexico (U.S. $102.6 billion), Argentina (U.S. $61.9 billion), Poland (U.S. $40.1 billion), and Venezuela (U.S. $34.1 billion).[3] While Canada's external debt is large in absolute terms, it is less imposing in relative terms. As a share of GDP, net debt in Canada at 35 percent is much lower than Mexico (58 percent in 1988), Argentina (60.5 percent), Poland (63.9 percent), and Venezuela (57.7 percent), but higher than only Brazil (30.7 percent). Canada has a larger external debt, but it is better able to service its debt than many other debtor nations.

Net indebtedness in Canada is continuing to grow more rapidly than GDP because of the persistence of current account deficits, whereas the other large debtors are being forced by lenders to reduce their net indebtedness relative to GDP. Canada's debt service ratio (investment income divided by exports) at 13.6 percent is in the same range as those of heavily indebted developing countries which are not experiencing debt-servicing difficulties (average 14.7 percent in 1989). It is well below those of developing countries experiencing debt-servicing difficulties (average 25.6 percent in 1989).

Interestingly, if Quebec's share of Canada's external indebtedness were the same as its share of population, its net external indebtedness would be greater than that of Poland and Venezuela. Its indebtedness would also presumably be growing more quickly.

TABLE 25

CANADIAN CURRENT ACCOUNT BALANCE AND EXTERNAL DEBT

	1986	*1987*	*1988*	*1989*
Current Account Bal.				
Billions of Dollars	-10.2	-9.2	-10.2	-16.7
Percent of GDP	-2.0	-1.7	-1.7	-2.6
Investment Income				
Billions of Dollars	-16.4	-16.2	-18.9	-22.2
Percent of GDP	-3.2	-2.9	-3.1	-3.4
Percent of Exports	-11.9	-11.2	-11.9	-13.6
Net Int. Inv. Position				
Billions of Dollars	-180.8	-194.2	-204.6	-229.3
Percent of GDP	-35.8	-35.2	-33.9	-35.2
Percent of Exports	-130.9	-134.2	-128.9	-140.8

Source: Statistics Canada, *Canada's International Investment Position*, Catalogue 67-202.

This chapter raises some questions about the extent to which a sovereign Quebec would be able to generate a trade surplus to service its external debt. This issue should be addressed more thoroughly than is possible here. The first order of business would be to get Statistics Canada to see if it could prepare estimates of Quebec's external balance and external indebtedness by using the raw statistical data it uses in preparing the national estimates. If so, then it would be possible to examine Quebec's ability to service this debt by drawing on its current industrial base. Attention should focus on the extent to which the narrower industrial base of Quebec and the economic fluctuation within its key industries might compromise its ability to service the debt.

Economic comparisons with the rest of Canada

There has been much talk about the dynamism of the Quebec economy and the new breed of Quebec entrepreneurs. It is important to remember, however, that Quebec remains one of Canada's less well off equalization receiving provinces. This relative lack of economic clout would not preclude Quebec from going on its own, but it would make it more difficult.

Table 26 shows that GDP per capita in Quebec in 1989 is $22,684, which is 88 percent of the average in the rest of Canada, or 79 percent of Ontario, the province with which Quebec usually makes comparisons. Similarly, personal income per capita is $19,614, which is 91 percent of the rest of Canada, or 82 percent of Ontario. Personal disposable income (after direct taxes) is $15,110, which is 88 percent of the rest of Canada, or 80 percent of Ontario. Earned income per capita is $15,718, which is 89 percent of the rest of Canada, or 82 percent of Ontario. The gap is smaller for the average wage (wages and salaries per employee). The average wage in Quebec was 96 percent of the rest of Canada, or 87 percent of Ontario.

TABLE 26

THE QUEBEC ECONOMY COMPARED TO THE REST OF CANADA IN 1989
(Dollars)

	Canada	Quebec	Ontario	Rest of Canada including Ontario
Population (thousands)	26,223	6,692	9,579	19,531
GDP per capita	24,896	22,684	28,537	25,653
Personal Income per capita	21,093	19,614	24,017	21,599
Personal Disp. Inc. per capita	16,638	15,110	18,809	17,161
Earned Income per capita	17,131	15,718	19,096	17,615
Average Wage	28,744	27,883	32,001	29,017
Employment (thousands) December 1990	12,439	2,999	4,867	9,440
Unemployment Rate (%) December 1990	9.3	11.7	7.8	8.6

Source: Statistics Canada. All figures are annual averages except for employment and unemployment rate which are for December 1990.

The relatively weak position of Quebec is also apparent in the labour market. At the end of 1990, the unemployment rate in Quebec was 11.7 percent, more than 3 percentage points higher than in the rest of the country and almost 4 percentage points higher than in Ontario. The disadvantage is even greater if a comparison is made between the proportions of the populations that are employed. In Quebec only 44.8 percent of the population is employed, versus 48.3 percent in the rest of Canada and 50.8 percent in Ontario.

International economic comparisons of GDP and population

An international comparison of population and income in 1988 is provided in table 27. Quebec would certainly not be the smallest country in the Organization for Economic Cooperation and Development if it were to become independent. Measured by GNP in U.S. dollars in 1988 converted at the average exchange rate, it would only be slightly smaller than Austria and larger than Denmark, Finland, and Norway. In terms of population Quebec would fit in between the same countries. Quebec's GDP per capita in U.S. dollars calculated at $17,421 would place it thirteenth among the 24 countries belonging to the OECD. Using purchasing power parity exchange rates to calculate GDP per capita, which provides a more accurate estimate of living standards than actual market exchange rates, Quebec would rank third behind only the United States and the rest of Canada.

The rest of Canada would remain the seventh largest economy in the OECD measured by GNP in U.S. dollars. Canada would thus still remain one of the world's seven largest industrial economies even if Quebec were to separate, but Spain would not be far behind.
Arithmetically, GDP per capita in Canada would increase with the separation of Quebec because GDP per capita in the rest of Canada is higher than in Quebec. By using purchasing power parity exchange rates, Canada would remain right at the top in terms of GDP per capita calculated, falling only behind the United States.

TABLE 27

INTERNATIONAL COMPARISON OF GNP AND POPULATION IN 1988
(U.S. Dollars)

Country	Population (Millions)	GNP/GDP$ (US$ Billions)	GNP/GDP Current Exchange Rate	Per Capita Purchasing Power Parity Exchange Rate
United States	246.329	4817.800	19,558	19,558
Japan	122.613	2843.400	23,190	14,288
Germany	61.451	1201.800	19,581	14,161
France	55.873	949.900	17,002	13,603
Italy	57.441	828.900	14,430	12,985
United Kingdom	57.065	822.800	14,413	13,428
Canada	**25.909**	**490.310**	**18,924**	**18,692**
Rest of Canada	**19.268**	**374.617**	**19,442**	**19,204**
Spain	38.996	340.100	8,722	9,343
Australia	16.538	247.100	14,940	13,412
Netherlands	14.765	228.300	15,461	12,832
Switzerland	6.672	183.700	27,581	16,700
Sweden	8.438	181.800	21,546	14,772
Belgium	9.879	150.000	15,180	12,623
Austria	7.595	127.200	16,748	12,506
Quebec	**6.641**	**115.692**	**17,421**	**17,207**
Denmark	5.130	107.500	20,912	13,555
Finland	4.946	105.200	21,266	13,792
Norway	4.211	91.200	21,654	16,322
Turkey	53.969	70.600	1,303	4,353
Greece	10.010	52.500	5,244	6,799
New Zealand	3.326	41.800	12,555	11,028
Portugal	10.304	41.700	4,265	6,750
Ireland	3.538	32.500	9,182	8,146
Luxembourg	0.375	6.600	17,592	15,558
Iceland	0.250	5.900	23,936	16,068

Source: OECD, *OECD Observer*, No. 164 (June/July 1990) and Statistics Canada, *Provincial Economic Accounts*, annual estimates 1985-89. Purchasing Power Parity Exchange rates for the rest of Canada and Quebec were assumed to be the same as those estimated for Canada by the OECD.

Fiscal deficits and public debt of a sovereign Quebec

The annual budget of Quebec provides the best accounting of the fiscal position of the province. Table 28 provides the Quebec government's budget forecast and some historical background on deficits and debt. The Liberal government has been successful since it came to power in 1985 in halving the deficit and financial requirements by 1989-90. The decline in the deficit slowed the growth of the public debt and brought down the public debt as a proportion of GDP from 29.3 percent in 1985-86 to 27.7 percent in 1989-90. Due to the recession, the deficit rose in 1990-91. and the debt-to-GDP ratio increased to 29 percent. This increase is projected to continue in 1991-92, but at nowhere near the rate that the deficit is projected to increase in Ontario.

To estimate the budgetary deficit of a sovereign Quebec, add the estimated provincial deficit in 1991-92 of $3.5 billion to Quebec's share of the estimated federal budgetary deficit of $7.8 billion ($30.5 billion times 25.4 percent population share). This calculation gives an estimated budgetary deficit for a sovereign Quebec of $11.3 billion. While a deficit of this magnitude may appear at first glance to be a crippling burden, it is not very much higher than the $9.7 billion deficit expected by Ontario in 1991-92. But this estimate of a sovereign Quebec's budget deficit is an underestimate since Quebec's share of the deficit may be larger than its share of population because it derives a net benefit from transactions with the federal government. Also, Quebec does not have the same capacity as Ontario to carry additional debt.

An additional source of data on Quebec's fiscal position is provided by the provincial economic accounts. Net lending or borrowing by the government sector in the provincial economic accounts gives another measure of the provincial deficit or surplus. The provincial economic accounts are also useful in that they show net lending or borrowing of the federal government in Quebec. Combining the federal with the other levels of government yields an estimate of what the national accounts

TABLE 28

QUEBEC BUDGET FORECAST 1991-92
(Millions of Dollars)

	1985-86	*1989-90*	*1990-91*	*1991-92*
Budgetary Deficit	3,344	1,659	2,795	3,480
Financial Requirements	1,671	816	1,482	2,200
Public Debt				
Direct	23,633	27,699	29,616	
Pension Funds	7,998	14,320	16,224	
Total	31,631	42,019	45,840	
Debt/GDP (%)	29.3	27.7	29.0	30.8
Public Debt Charges as percent of Revenue	14	13.2	13.4	13.6

Source: Quebec, Ministry of Finance (1991, Annex B).

deficit of the Quebec government would be if it were to raise all the revenues in the province and carry out all of the expenditures of government in the province. This estimate is, in effect, what the Quebec government deficit would be on a national accounts basis if it were sovereign and continued with all existing programs and taxes.

Table 29 shows that the provincial-local deficit on a provincial accounts basis has declined similarly to the public accounts deficit presented in the provincial budget; in 1989, it was $1.4 billion, or less than 1 percent of GDP. The federal government deficit in Quebec has also declined, but much less significantly. In 1989, it was $5 billion, or 3.3 percent of GDP. Combining these two deficits, the deficit of a sovereign Quebec would have been $6.4 billion in 1989, or 4.2 percent of GDP. (Note that the estimated Quebec government deficit on a provincial economic accounts basis is lower than the estimate on a public accounts basis for the same reasons that federal national accounts deficits are lower than federal budgetary deficits. For example, contributions to public service superannuation accounts are counted as revenues in the national accounts.)

TABLE 29

QUEBEC DEFICITS ESTIMATED FROM PROVINCIAL ECONOMIC ACCOUNTS

	1986	1987	1988	1989
Provincial-Local Govts.				
-millions of dollars	-2327	-1643	-105	-1425
-percent of GDP	-2.0	-1.3	-0.1	-0.9
Federal Government				
-millions of dollars	-5673	-4524	-4480	-4968
-percent of GDP	-4.8	-3.5	-3.1	-3.3
Total Government				
-millions of dollars	-8000	-6167	-4585	-6393
-percent of GDP	-6.8	-4.8	-3.2	-4.2

Source: Net lending of governments from Statistics Canada, *Provincial Economic Accounts*.

Table 30 shows the revenues and expenditures that underlie the Quebec deficit on a provincial economic accounts basis and compares the revenues, expenditures, and the balance with that in the rest of Canada and Ontario. In 1989, Quebec's deficit (4.2 percent of GDP) was larger than the rest of Canada's (3.3 percent of GDP) and especially larger than Ontario's (with running a surplus of 1.7 percent of GDP). The favourable fiscal position of Ontario is not expected to persist in light of the dramatic increase in the provincial government deficit forecast in the 1991 budget. Quebec's revenue share at 41.7 percent of GDP was significantly higher than the rest of Canada's (40.2 percent) and Ontario's (40.4 percent). Its expenditure share at 45.9 percent of GDP is also significantly above the rest of Canada's (43.3 percent) and especially above Ontario's (38.8 percent). Again, the 1991 Ontario budget will change this comparison.

TABLE 30

COMPARISON OF GOVERNMENT REVENUE, EXPENDITURES AND NET LENDING IN 1989
(Percent of GDP)

	Canada	Quebec	Ontario	Rest of Canada including Ontario
Revenue	40.5	41.7	40.4	40.2
Expenditure	43.9	45.9	38.8	43.3
Net Lending	-3.5	-4.2	1.7	-3.3

Source: Statistics Canada, *Provincial Economic Accounts*.

A sovereign Quebec would have to raise taxes or cut spending significantly to reduce its deficit. The deficit reduction would have to be at least equal to 1 percent of GDP, or $1.5 billion, to bring the deficit more into line with deficits in the rest of the country. Additional reductions in the deficit would be necessary to cover the loss of the federal fiscal benefits (1.25 to 2 percent of GDP) and to cover increased debt service. The debt service would increase if Quebec assumed a per capita share of federal debt (0.7 percent of GDP), if the risk premium on interest costs increased due to the large increment in Quebec government debt (0.2 percent of GDP assuming an 0.25 percent premium), and if taxes decreased because of any long-run declines in real output. These changes would add up to a total required reduction in the deficit of 2 to 3 percent of GDP, which is, coincidentally, roughly the same order of magnitude as the estimated required decrease in the current account deficit. If Quebec were to raise taxes by this magnitude, Quebeckers would have to reduce their spending significantly. There is also a risk that large tax increases would undermine Quebec's competitiveness. On the other hand, cuts in spending would reduce services to Quebec citizens.

It is possible to do some rough calculations of the debt burden of a sovereign Quebec. At the end of 1990-91, the gross public debt of the Quebec government, excluding debt held by retirement plan accounts, was equal to 18.8 percent of GDP. The net public debt of Quebec local governments was $16,250 million in 1990 or 10.3 percent of GDP.[4] Federal gross public debt at the end of 1990-91 would be approximately $430 billion (estimated by adding the difference between 1989-90 gross and net public debt to the 1990-91 net public debt of $388.5 billion estimated in the 1991 federal budget). Federal gross public debt excluding pension liabilities would be $359 billion (estimated by subtracting the 1989-90 estimate of federal pension liabilities of $71 billion from $430 billion), or 58 percent of GDP. The total gross public debt of a sovereign Quebec would thus be 87.1 percent of GDP, excluding the debt held by retirement plans (the sum of the provincial debt of 18.8 percent, local debt of 10.3 percent, and the share of federal debt of 58 percent). This rough measure of Quebec's gross debt burden is reasonably comparable with the gross public debt (excluding debt held in pension accounts) of other major industrialized countries compiled by the OECD shown in table 31. If Quebec were sovereign, it would have a larger gross public debt than Canada and any of the six other largest industrialized countries except for Italy. Of the smaller countries only Belgium and Ireland would have higher gross debt. A sovereign Quebec would definitely be a high public debt country.

Further light on the issue of the debt burden of a sovereign Quebec is shed by considering recent estimates of provincial-local net debt prepared by Irene Ip of the C.D. Howe Institute (Ip, 1991). Net debt differs from gross debt in that it is measured after subtracting financial assets. These estimates, which were painstakingly constructed to be interprovincially comparable, are given in table 32. According to these estimates for 1989, Quebec, with net debt equal to 35.1 percent of GDP, is, after Newfoundland, the most heavily indebted province in relative terms. Its debt was 24 percent of GDP higher than Ontario's and 25 percent of GDP higher than the rest of Canada's average for provincial-local debt.

Ip estimates that if federal debt were allocated to Quebec based on population, the combined debt ratio in Quebec would be 95 percent. In contrast, the combined debt ratio for the rest of Canada would only be 63.3 percent (calculated using Ip's data). By this measure, if Quebec were to separate and assume its per capita share of the federal public debt, Quebec would have a 50 percent higher debt burden than the rest of Canada.

TABLE 31

GROSS PUBLIC DEBT IN 1991
(Percent of GDP)

Country	Debt/GDP
United States	54.8
Japan	61.3
Germany	47.0
France	46.5
Italy	101.0
United Kingdom	34.2
Canada	73.0
Total G-7	57.4
Australia	7.2
Austria	54.0
Belgium	129.3
Denmark	55.8
Finland	13.0
Greece	86.5
Ireland	113.1
Netherlands	84.6
Norway	39.5
Spain	43.0
Sweden	40.9
Total Small Countries	54.8
Total	57.1

Source: OECD, *Economic Outlook*, December 1990.

Fiscal comparisons with other provinces

A comparison of consolidated provincial-local government fiscal balances in 1989 as a percent of GDP on a Financial Management System basis using data prepared by Irene Ip (1991, Table A6) is provided in Figure 3. On this basis, Quebec's deficit was smaller relative to GDP than Nova Scotia's and Alberta's, but larger than the other provinces', particularly Ontario's which ran a surplus. However, a continuation of a high rate of spending growth in Ontario in the face of a recession is expected to push the Ontario budget deeply into deficit beginning in 1991. Quebec will not continue to record a larger deficit than Ontario, but should remain higher than most of the other provinces.

TABLE 32

PROVINCIAL-LOCAL NET DEBT IN 1989
(Percent of GDP)

Newfoundland	42.2
Quebec[a]	35.1
Nova Scotia	29.3
New Brunswick	25.8
Manitoba	25.3
Prince Edward Island	14.9
Saskatchewan	13.8
Ontario	11.1
British Columbia	4.9
Alberta	-6.0
Total Prov.-Local	15.9
Total Prov.-Local ex. Quebec	10.1
Federal	54.9
Total	70.8

[a]Excludes QPP assets for sake of comparability.

Source: Irene Ip (1991, Table A.5). Provincial debt is as of March 31, 1990; local debt as of December 31, 1989.

An important indicator of the strength of fiscal position is public debt charges as a percentage of revenue or the interest/revenue ratio. It is the inverse of the interest coverage ratio. Figure 4 shows that public debt charges in Quebec in 1990-91 were higher than in other provinces except for Newfoundland and Nova Scotia (Department of Finance, 1991b, p.19).

FIGURE 3

CONSOLIDATED PROVINCIAL-LOCAL SURPLUS/DEFICIT (-) IN 1989

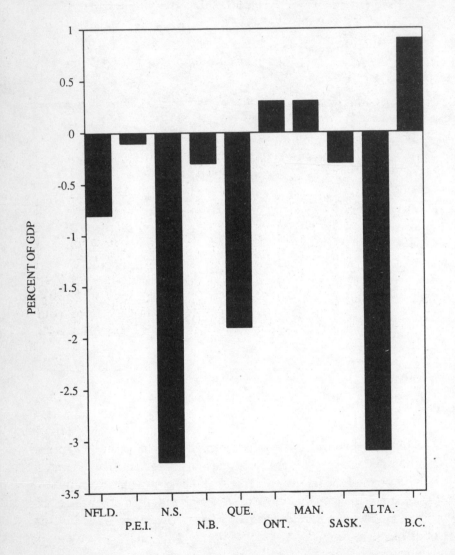

Source: Financial Management System Basis (Irene Ip, 1991, table A.6)

FIGURE 4

PUBLIC DEBT CHARGES AS A PERCENT OF REVENUE IN 1990-91

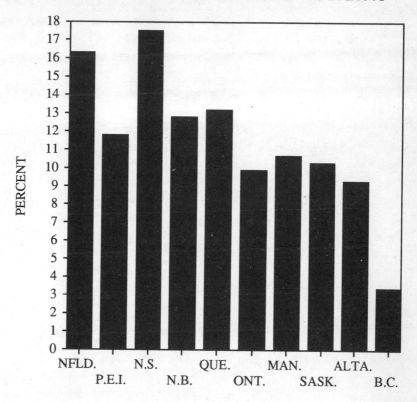

Source: Department of Finance (1991b, p. 19).

Given that a sovereign Quebec would have to raise significantly more revenue than it does currently, it is important to consider its revenue-raising capability in relation to those of the other provinces. Several measures can be used to compare the abilities of the provinces to raise revenues. The first measure is the relative "fiscal capacity" of a province, which measures the ability of a province to get revenue from available sources. It is calculated both for own-source revenues and own-source revenues plus equalization. The second is the relative "tax effort" of a province, which measures the revenue that a province raises relative to the revenue it would raise if it were to levy taxes at the national average provincial tax rates. These measures were provided by the Federal Provincial Relations Division of the Department of Finance in June 1991.

The measure of relative fiscal capacity from own sources is shown in table 33. It is estimated for each province by taking the per capita yield of own-source revenues from a standardized tax system, which applies a uniform tax rate to a uniform tax base for each revenue source. Own-source revenue excludes interest revenues of provincial governments, all non-tax revenues of local governments, and federal transfer payments.

The large variation in relative fiscal capacity from own source revenues across provinces and the stability in recent years of the provincial positions is evident from the table. Quebec has a fiscal capacity greater than the Atlantic provinces' and Manitoba's, but 14 percent less than Canada's average and 21 percent less than Ontario's. Because of oil and gas revenues, Alberta has a strong position with an index of 134.5 percent. While Alberta's index is down from well over 200 percent in the late 1970s, it is still head and shoulders above the other provinces and more than twice as high as the indexes of Newfoundland and Prince Edward Island, the lowest income provinces.

Table 34 shows that equalization substantially reduces the disparity in fiscal capacity among provinces, bringing Quebec up to 92 percent of the national average. While Alberta remains the highest, the disparity among the other nine provinces decreases markedly when equalization is taken into account; it falls within an 11 percentage point range. Equalization brings all of the equalization receiving provinces up to the same level.

An indicator of tax effort is provided in table 35. It is calculated by dividing the revenues a province actually receives by the revenues that the representative tax system would yield in the province at average provincial rates. Tax effort varies considerably across provinces. Quebec has the highest level of tax effort at 111.2 percent; Alberta has the lowest level of tax effort at 74.4 percent. The Prairie provinces of Saskatchewan and Manitoba at 107.5 percent have relatively high levels of tax effort. The Atlantic provinces all have lower than average levels of tax effort. Ontario increased its level of tax effort from below the provincial average in 1987-88 to above the average in 1989-90, which is especially striking, given the importance of Ontario's tax increases in pulling up the national average. The decrease in the relatively high tax burden in Quebec during the same period is also noteworthy.

Nevertheless, in 1990 the tax burden in Quebec remained significantly higher than in Ontario. The top marginal personal income tax rate in Quebec in 1990 was 50.5 percent, compared to 48.2 percent in Ontario. Quebec's higher tax rate cost $964 more in income tax than Ontario's did for a couple with two children earning $50,000; and Quebec's cost $2,075 more than Ontario's for the same couple earning $75,000. A single individual would pay $540 more with an income of $20,000, $1,619 more at $35,000, $2,359 at $50,000, and $3,436 more at $75,000 (Quebec, 1990, pp.9-10). The differential would surely increase in a sovereign Quebec.

If tax effort were adjusted for the surpluses and deficits, the disparity in tax effort would widen since large deficits tend to be correlated with high tax effort. Unfortunately, data on the adjusted measure of tax effort are not available.

TABLE 33

INDICES OF PROVINCIAL LOCAL FISCAL CAPACITY OWN SOURCE REVENUES

	1987-88	*1988-89*	*1989-90*	*1990-91*	*1991-92*
Newfoundland	60.4	62.4	62.7	62.4	63.1
Prince Edward Is.	64.1	65.0	64.4	63.8	64.6
Nova Scotia	76.0	75.3	74.9	75.0	75.6
New Brunswick	71.2	72.0	71.1	70.4	71.2
Quebec	85.4	85.7	86.0	85.6	86.1
Ontario	108.2	109.9	111.2	110.9	109.5
Manitoba	80.2	80.7	79.1	79.3	80.0
Saskatchewan	90.3	87.2	83.8	85.8	87.3
Alberta	145.6	136.5	130.5	133.0	134.5
British Columbia	103.9	105.2	106.5	105.2	104.9
All Provinces	100.0	100.0	100.0	100.0	100.0

Source: Federal Provincial Relations Division, Finance, April 1991.

TABLE 34

INDICES OF PROVINCIAL LOCAL FISCAL CAPACITY
OWN SOURCE REVENUES PLUS EQUALIZATION

	1987-88	1988-89	1989-90	1990-91	1991-92
Newfoundland	91.8	91.8	91.5	91.2	92.0
Prince Edward Is.	91.8	91.8	91.5	91.2	92.0
Nova Scotia	91.8	91.8	91.5	91.2	92.0
New Brunswick	91.8	91.8	91.5	91.2	92.0
Quebec	91.8	91.8	91.5	91.2	92.0
Ontario	101.3	103.0	104.3	104.2	102.8
Manitoba	91.8	91.8	91.5	91.2	92.0
Saskatchewan	91.8	91.8	91.5	91.2	92.0
Alberta	136.2	127.8	122.3	125.0	126.3
British Columbia	97.2	98.6	99.9	98.8	98.5
All Provinces	100.0	100.0	100.0	100.0	100.0

Source: Federal Provincial Relations Division, Finance, April 1991.

TABLE 35

INDICES OF PROVINCIAL-LOCAL TAX EFFORT
ACTUAL REVENUES AS A PERCENTAGE OF REVENUES
AT NATIONAL AVERAGE TAX RATES

	1987-88	1988-89	1989-90
Newfoundland	108.1	106.0	99.8
Prince Edward Island	95.2	96.0	92.1
Nova Scotia	94.7	91.4	90.4
New Brunswick	91.7	97.8	97.6
Quebec	118.9	116.1	111.2
Ontario	98.3	100.1	103.2
Manitoba	115.1	111.7	107.4
Saskatchewan	104.5	103.1	107.5
Alberta	77.4	72.4	74.4
British Columbia	92.4	96.9	93.1
All Provinces	100.0	100.0	100.0

Source: Estimate for 1989-90 calculated using data on equalization entitlements dated February 14, 1991 provided by Federal Provincial Relations Division, Finance. Estimates for earlier years provided in September 1990.

Provincial-local expenditure per capita for all provinces for the 1989 calendar year from the Provincial Economic Accounts (the latest year currently available on a consolidated basis) are given in table 36. The table also provides indexes of the ratio of per capita expenditures in a particular province to the average for Canada. The variation in per capita spending is much less than the variation in fiscal capacity. Provinces tend to provide broadly comparable levels of public services. According to this measure, the greatest expenditure effort is made by Alberta and the least by Prince Edward Island. The Prairie provinces as a group have above average expenditure indexes and the Atlantic provinces below average. Quebec has a level of expenditure effort that is 6 percent higher than the national average and 14.5 percent higher than Ontario's. Again, projected expenditure increases in the 1991 Ontario budget should narrow the gap.

TABLE 36

PROVINCIAL-LOCAL EXPENDITURE PER CAPITA IN 1989

Province	$ Per Capita	Index
Alberta	7,175	119.0
Saskatchewan	6,787	112.6
Manitoba	6,491	107.7
Quebec	6,403	106.2
Newfoundland	5,732	95.1
Ontario	5,594	92.8
New Brunswick	5,416	89.9
British Columbia	5,407	89.7
Nova Scotia	5,384	89.3
Prince Edward Island	5,169	85.8
Canada average	6,027	100.0

Source: Statistics Canada, *Provincial Economic Accounts*

The impact of uncertainty over sovereignty on Quebec's borrowing costs

Financial markets pass judgment every day on the credit of borrowers. The yield on Quebec government bonds reflects yields on competing securities and the market's assessment of the appropriate risk premium for Quebec bonds. This assessment takes into account the prospects for Quebec, including the possibility of sovereignty and any difficulties in servicing the debt which could result. Using a series prepared by Richardson Greenshields for the Caisse de dépôt, an examination of the interest rate gap between Quebec and Canada long-term bonds over the last twenty years reveals that the gap widens during recessions and during periods of political uncertainty (figure 5). Recessions have been the most important factor causing increases in the gap. But it would be difficult to deny that political uncertainties have played some role.[5] It is difficult to identify clearly the separate effect of political uncertainty.

In the period leading up to the June 23, 1990 Meech Lake deadline and immediately after, the yield on Canadian long-term bonds increased by almost 1.5 percentage points more than the yield on comparable U.S. bonds. The Bank of Canada in its annual report attributes some of this increase to political uncertainty (Bank of Canada, 1990, p.29). Furthermore, as support in Quebec for sovereignty has gathered momentum since the failure of Meech Lake last summer, the gap between Quebec and Canada long bonds increased by about 50 basis points, from about 90 basis points to a peak of almost 140 basis points (figure 6). This gap was about 25 basis points more than the gap between Ontario and Canada long bonds. More recently (as of July 13), the gap has narrowed again to around 80 basis points as support for sovereignty has waned in the polls.

While it is not easy to interpret these changes, the market seems to be signalling that, while an independent Quebec may be viable, its debt is riskier than if it were to remain part of Canada. Also, Quebec would have to pay an interest premium for sovereignty. The reasons that the market might require such a premium should be evident from this paper's discussions of Quebec's fiscal deficits, its debt and external balances, and its industrial structure. It is not surprising that the Canadian Bond Rating Service announced in March that, even though it was not downgrading Quebec's credit rating from AA, it was putting all bonds issued by the Quebec government and its agencies on credit watch (Milner and Seguin, 1990, pp.A1-A2). There is just too much uncertainty about Quebec's future prospects. In contrast, Moody's has adopted a more cautious approach and announced that it will not alter Quebec's credit rating until there is "a formal adoption by the Quebec government of a series of constitutional reforms" (McKenna, 1991, p.B8).

An overall assessment of the viability of a sovereign Quebec

It cannot be denied that a sovereign Quebec would be viable economically. Quebec would not be the smallest country in the OECD if it were to become independent. Measured by GNP in U.S. dollars in 1988 converted at the average exchange rate, it would only be slightly smaller than Austria and larger than Denmark, Finland, and Norway. In population, Quebec would fit in between the same countries. Quebec's GNP per capita in terms of U.S. dollar purchasing power parity at $17,207 would place it as the third highest income of OECD countries, behind the United States and Canada.

Quebec is currently going through the same recession as the rest of the Canadian economy. However, the confidence of Quebeckers in the economic viability of sovereign Quebec has evidently not yet been shaken as it was in the 1981-82 recession following the 1980 referendum. Prospects are good for a strong recovery beginning in the summer of 1991, assuming that Quebec remains part of Canada and the economic upheaval associated with separation is thereby avoided. The best time to consider subjecting the Quebec economy to the shock of separation from Canada is not during a recession, even though the Quebec economy is viable.

The Quebec economy has several weaknesses which would be exacerbated by independence. The budgetary deficit of the Quebec government would increase to more than $10 billion if Quebec were to take over the existing federal structure of revenues and expenditures. The deficit on a provincial economic accounts basis would be $6.5 billion, or 4.2 percent of GDP.

FIGURE 5

GAP BETWEEN THE RATE OF RETURN ON LONG-TERM BONDS OF HYDRO-QUEBEC AND GOVERNMENT OF CANADA

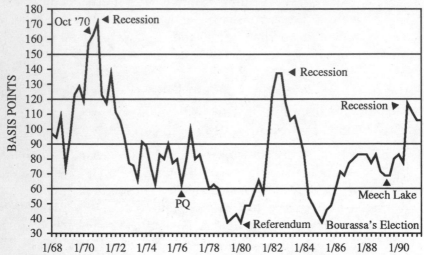

Source: Richardson Greenshields.

Net public debt as a proportion of GDP would rise from 35 percent of GDP in 1989 to 95 percent if Quebec's share of federal net debt based on population were factored in. Quebec would have a larger gross public debt than any of the seven largest industrialized countries except for Italy. Of the smaller countries considered, only Belgium and Ireland would have higher gross debt. A sovereign Quebec would definitely be a high public debt country. Slower population growth would make it more difficult for Quebec to bear its share of the debt than for the rest of Canada.

International and domestic lenders could be expected to exact an interest premium from the Quebec government to compensate for the greater risk of lending to a high-debt sovereign Quebec, as they were doing until recently when support for sovereignty began to wane. The benefits Quebec would be giving up in terms of greater stability of revenues resulting from federal transfers are evidently recognized by lenders.

In addition, Quebec's external position would appear to be weak. Although in 1984 (the latest year for which data are available) Quebec

FIGURE 6

RECENT INTEREST RATE GAPS BETWEEN HYDRO-QUÉBEC AND GOVERNMENT OF CANADA BONDS

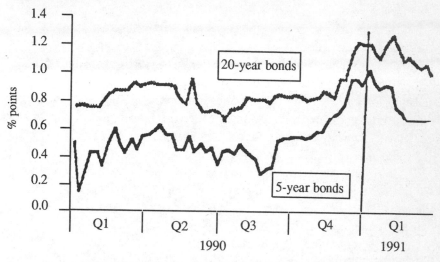

Source: Reuters Historical Information, *Globe and Mail*, March 27, 1991, p. B4.

had a surplus of $3.3 billion in its trade in manufactured goods with the rest of Canada, its overall trade balance was in deficit by $4.2 billion, or 4.2 percent of GDP. And, $1.9 billion (or 56 percent) of the surplus in interprovincial trade in manufactured goods was concentrated in the five "soft" industries of leather and allied products, primary textiles, textile products, clothing, and furniture and fixtures. These industries are labour-intensive and subject to strong foreign competition. The most important of these, textiles and clothing, benefits from access to a protected Canadian market guarded by high tariffs and quotas which could not be expected to continue if Quebec were to become sovereign. Quebec's dairy farmers, who supply almost one-half of Canada's industrial milk and who benefit from supply management, might also suffer a substantial loss in market share.[6] Moreover, Quebec's international exports of manufactured goods, which are concentrated in paper and allied products, primary metals, and transportation equipment, are also vulnerable. Paper and allied products is currently suffering from the recession and from recycling. Transportation equipment would depend on Quebec's continued participation in the auto pact. Of Quebec's exports, only hydroelectricity is an unambiguous source of strength, but even it could be affected by territorial disputes with Canada or the James Bay Cree and by any efforts by Newfoundland to cut off Churchill Falls's power.

Data from the provincial economic accounts also suggest that Quebec's external position would be much weaker than Canada's. A sovereign Quebec could have trouble servicing its external debt if it did not take steps to strengthen its current account balance and to compress real incomes of Quebeckers. Quebec industry would have to adjust more quickly to meet international competition. A rough estimate of the required transfer of resources to the external sector would be two to three percent of GDP.

And this estimate assumes that Quebec would maintain a common currency with Canada. The establishment of a separate currency would increase transactions costs in trade with the rest of Canada and add to the nervousness of investors, thereby making it harder to service Quebec's large, though yet unmeasured, external debt. A separate currency would also make it more difficult for Quebec to pick up its share of the federal public debt; it would add an element of currency risk to the risk premium in interest rates. On the other hand, a devaluation of a Quebec currency may turn out to be the easiest way to get the Quebec public to accept lower real incomes.

This estimate also assumes that Quebec would be able to negotiate free trade agreements with the rest of Canada and the United States. This assumption is reasonable enough in the medium term after enough time has elapsed for agreements to be reached. But there could very well be costs for Quebec. The agreements, once they are reached, may not be as favourable to Quebec as current agreements are. The United States and Canada could both demand limitations on the extent to which Quebec would be able to pursue interventionist policies in support of domestic industries. Quebec government procurement policies which favour domestic suppliers and subsidized hydroelectricity are two possible sources of contention. The use of the Caisse de dépôt to promote the development of Quebec industry and the environmental consequences of James Bay II could also become sources of disagreement.

And the United States could also pursue its longstanding grievances over trade in alcoholic beverages and agricultural supply management.

Even though a sovereign Quebec would be viable, the government of the new state would have to embark on a structural adjustment program as its first order of business. It would have to reduce the government deficit by two to three percent of GDP. To resolve emerging structural disquilibria in the fiscal and trade balances and to gain the confidence of international investors, it would have to improve the current account balance by two to three percent of GDP. These reductions would require substantial cuts in government spending, resulting in lower levels of government services. The reductions might also entail increases in taxes. But the government would have to tread softly in hiking taxes as Quebec's tax burden is already significantly higher than the rest of Canada's and much higher than the United States'. Relying too heavily on tax increases would risk further undermining the competitiveness of Quebec industry. Reducing the government deficit would help to improve Quebec's current account deficit. The Quebec government would also have to facilitate the transfer of resources out of the "soft" industries. A free trade agreement with Canada and the United States would be essential if Quebec is to remain as prosperous as today.

A sovereign Quebec may be viable economically, but the economic policies required to ensure viability will require some very difficult structural adjustments and some unpopular policy-induced reductions in real incomes. The heavy cloud of uncertainty over the prospects of Quebec's economy was underlined by the Canadian Bond Rating Agency in its March announcement that it was putting all bonds issued by the Quebec government and its agencies on credit watch. It is surprising that the large international bond rating agencies, such as Moodys and Standard and Poors, have not echoed the concerns of the Canadian Bond Rating Agency. But they are not located in Montreal and are more distant from the scene.

The real question for Quebeckers is not whether they would be better off economically—because economics is not their sole motive for independence—but whether they are willing to pay substantially for independence. The next chapter brings together all the arguments as to why Quebeckers, and indeed all Canadians, would be worse off if Quebec were to separate.

Notes

1. This argument was made first and in more detail by Reuven Brenner (1991, pp.7-9).

2. The Department of Finance (1991c) has prepared a useful study of economic linkages among provinces which also examines trade flows.

3. Data on debt of other countries are taken from IMF (1990) and World Bank (1990).

4. The unpublished data on Quebec local government debt in 1990 were provided by the Public Institutions Division of Statistics Canada.

5. Montmarquette and Dallaire (1980) examined the increase in differentials in interest rate in Quebec and Ontario bonds after the 1976 PQ election using econometric techniques. Their conclusions were that the present value of the additional financing costs was 1.22 percent of the $2,656 million in borrowings over the November 1976 to February 1979 period and that it took two and a half years for the difference in financing costs to disappear. Boothe and Harris (1991, p.21) attempted to isolate sovereign risk premiums by comparing U.S. pay bonds for Canada, Alberta, B.C. Hydro, Hydro-Quebec, and Ontario with a U.S. Treasury bond of comparable maturity and coupon over the 1986 to 1991 period. While the risk premium has narrowed since the beginning of the year, Quebec-Hydro bonds, which in March 1991 were 100 basis points over U.S. Treasury's and 80 basis point over Canada's, traded at the highest risk premium since early 1990 of all the bonds considered.

6. Murray Smith estimates that the tariff equivalent of the dairy supply management regime is 50 to 70 percent (Smith, 1991, p.5).

Chapter 5

The bottom line for Quebec sovereignty

Canada's prosperity threatened by Quebec sovereignty

QUEBEC SOVEREIGNTY HAS MANY possibly dire economic consequences for Canada, especially for Quebec. Few would deny that Canada has been an economic success story. International leaders such as U.S. President George Bush and German Chancellor Helmut Kohl have taken the unusual step of expressing their concerns about a breakup of Canada (Beltrame, 1991 and Drohan, 1991). Although small in population, Canada has the seventh largest economy in the OECD. Canada's standard of living is the second highest after the United States. Canada is richly endowed with resources and has a diversified industrial economy. Drawn by our prosperity, immigrants from all over the world flock to Canada. Quebec has flourished economically in Canada; Quebeckers have shared in the bountiful income and wealth generated by the Canadian economy.

Canada has been doing well. Granted, Canada can do better, but it can also do much worse. Breaking Quebec off from one of the world's strongest economies is unquestionably a way to do worse.

Since Quebec sovereignty threatens our hard-won economic success, both Canadians and Quebeckers need to understand fully its economic consequences. The negotiation of trade agreements, the transition costs and the long-run economic impacts—all of these issues must be considered to gain a proper appreciation of the economic consequences of Quebec sovereignty.

Sovereignty-association is a non-starter

Quebec is an integral part of the Canadian economy. Even if Quebec were to separate, bidirectional flows of goods and services, capital and labour would have to be maintained. Continued trade would require some accommodation on both sides, but Quebec would be wrong to assume that Canada has no choice but to negotiate economic association on Quebec's terms. The backlash in the rest of Canada from Quebec's separation and hard-ball bargaining on both sides could easily lead to a mutually destructive trade war.

Sovereignty-association seems to be the preferred option of many Québécois for economic relationships with the rest of Canada. It has the attraction of preserving the continued free circulation of people and goods between Canada and Quebec. The two pillars of sovereignty-association are a customs union and a monetary union.

No customs union

The existing Canadian customs union has evolved over years in response to the shifting balance of regional and sectoral economic and political forces. It would be highly unrealistic to expect it to persist if political ties between Quebec and Canada were ruptured. Its continuation requires a federal government for resolving disputes. There can be no economic union without a political union.

Moreover, if Quebec were to separate, a continued customs union would not necessarily be in Canada's self-interest. A customs union would require Canada to give up control over its external tariff and to adopt a common commercial policy. But it would not make economic sense for Canada to retain the same duties on clothing, textiles and footwear as Quebec, where more than half of the industry is centred.

For the rest of Canada, interprovincial trade in textiles and clothing represents economic welfare reducing trade diversion and not welfare increasing trade creation.

The textile and clothing industries, which are the largest and most important of Quebec's "soft" industries. are able to operate only behind high tariff walls and, even then, only after being propped up by Voluntary Export Restraints (VER) under the Multi-Fibre Agreement (MFA). Effective rates of protection for textiles average 16.6 percent; Most Favoured Nation (MFN) customs tariffs for most clothing are 25 percent. Import penetration in the market for textiles and clothing has been limited to 30 to 33 percent through restraints on 80 percent of imports.

Other contentious trade issues would have to be resolved to maintain a customs union with Canada. Quebec's dairy farmers supply almost half of Canada's industrial milk at inflated prices under the shield of supply management marketing boards. As a result, Quebec has a trade surplus with the rest of Canada of more than $700 million in dairy products, not including fluid milk. Quebec-Hydro, benefiting from a long-term contract with Newfoundland, reportedly resells Churchill Falls's power for $800 million per year profit (Gorham, 1991, p.E6). Neither of these situations would be allowed to continue if Quebec were to become a foreign country and trade regulations were to change.

In a Canada without Quebec, Western Canada, which traditionally supports free trade and criticizes the way resource industries are treated would be more influential in the determination of national trade policy. Quebec's departure would break the Ontario-Quebec axis in support of manufacturing.

A free trade agreement would probably be about as far as Canada would want to go to accommodate Quebec. And this agreement would not be an act of magnanimity; it would be in Canada's interest. But it would require Canadians to put aside any hard feelings resulting from a break and could thus not be considered a certainty.

Under a free trade agreement there would have to be border control points between Canada and Quebec to enforce rules of origin and commodity taxes. Even in the European Economic Community there are still border controls on the flow of goods.

Trade arrangements with Canada would not be the only difficulty facing Quebec. The Canada-United States Free Trade Agreement would not automatically apply to an independent Quebec. While the United States would probably be receptive, Quebec would still have to negotiate its own agreement. There is no guarantee that a new agreement would be as favourable as the existing Canada-United States Agreement. As a Canadian province, Quebec has been spared the full extent of scrutiny by U.S. trade negotiators. Government procurement could become a target. Trade barriers affecting alcoholic beverages and agricultural supply management could come under renewed attack. The United States might also investigate the much heavier degree of government intervention under Quebec Inc. American negotiators may want to discuss low-cost electricity provided to industrial users such a Norsk Hydro (Globe and Mail, 1991) and the promotion of Quebec businesses by the Caisse de dépôt. They may even wish to negotiate environmental safeguards on the development of James Bay II. Even barring these contentious issues, the negotiation process would be time-consuming. Quebec could not expect to jump to the head of the United States' trade negotiation queue. The U.S. Congress would also want to make sure its views are reflected in any negotiations. All of this could take years and would contribute to a climate of uncertainty which would undermine economic performance.[1]

Maybe a monetary union

The Bélanger-Campeau Commission argued that the Canadian dollar could be maintained as a sovereign Quebec's currency through legislation declaring the Canadian dollar legal tender in Quebec (Commission, 1991, p.58). Jacques Parizeau has gone even further: he said that Canada can do nothing to stop Quebec from using the currency (Macdonald, 1991). For Quebeckers worried about their life savings being eroded by a depreciating Quebec dollar, this could well be the deciding issue for Quebec sovereignty.

But Parizeau is wrong: If Quebec chooses to separate, there is no guarantee that it could continue to use the Canadian dollar. Only the Canadian government can run a Canadian dollar monetary system. It alone can print the currency that people want to hold and make the rules under which the payments system operates. While a quarter of the

Canadian money supply is now in Quebec, paper money wears out and must be replaced on a regular basis. The average life of $2, $5 and $10 bills is currently less than one year, and the average life of a $20 bill, less than two years. Only the Canadian government can supply replacement currency.

Even if Quebec were to separate amicably, problems would arise for Canada if Canada allowed Quebec to use the Canadian dollar. It would be impossible for the Canadian regulatory authorities to guarantee the solvency of the Canadian financial system if Quebec financial institutions could clear through the Canadian Payments Association and if the Office of the Supervisor of Financial Institutions did not have supervisory authority over them. The bankruptcy of a major Quebec institution could occur without warning and could bring down the Canadian financial institution with which it had clearing arrangements.

In addition, the Bank of Canada's conduct of monetary policy would be more difficult if a large proportion of Canadian currency and Canadian dollar bank accounts were outside its control. Unlike Canadian financial institutions, Quebec financial institutions could not be compelled to report regularly to the Bank of Canada. This would make it more difficult for the Bank of Canada to rely on current monetary indicators to gauge the stance of monetary policy. More importantly, monetary policy would have to be altered to respond to changes in the money supply caused by inflows and outflows of Canadian dollars from Quebec (resulting from, among other things, different macroeconomic policy stances in Quebec and Canada). This change could conflict with the domestic objectives of monetary policy, such as the pursuit of price stability.

A sovereign Quebec would also encounter problems if it used Canadian currency. The only way Quebec could acquire additional Canadian currency would be by running a balance of payments surplus, which would require either a current account surplus or an increase in foreign indebtedness. Ultimately, Quebec would have to transfer real resources to Canada in exchange for paper currency.

If Quebec were to separate on acrimonious terms and try to avoid bearing its share of the public debt, the reaction of the rest of Canada would be understandably hostile. In that situation, there are some, admittedly extreme, steps that the Canadian government could take to prevent Quebec from using the Canadian dollar. Existing Canadian currency could be recalled and new notes issued. Restrictions could be put on the export of Canadian currency. Regulations could be established to deny Quebec financial institutions direct access to the Canadian Payments Association.

Such extreme measures would only be taken if there was a complete breakdown of relations between Quebec and the rest of Canada. But Quebeckers must know that they would not hold all the trump cards in negotiations with Canada if bargaining were to get really tough.

Even in a climate of good faith bargaining, a monetary union between Quebec and Canada would be hard to sell to the rest of Canada. To persuade English Canadians of the need for a monetary union, Quebeckers could appeal to English Canadians' pocket books: they could argue that a monetary union was necessary for Quebec to assume its share of the Canadian dollar denominated public debt. Obviously, Quebec would experience more difficulties in carrying its share of the debt load if it had its own currency. But Quebec would have to accept its fair share of the federal government debt as a *quid pro quo* for a monetary union.

English Canada could be expected to embrace a monetary union with Quebec only reluctantly, if at all, and to yield little, if any, say in the formulation of monetary policy to a sovereign Quebec. Other provinces would find it very difficult to accept Quebec representation on the central bank if they were excluded. In addition, even if a monetary union were established, it might not last. In the past, monetary unions without political unions have always eventually collapsed (Howitt, 1991, p.22).

If no agreement were reached on a monetary union, the lack of a common currency between Canada and Quebec would be more troublesome for Quebec than Canada. The smaller and more open an economy is and the less diversified and the more variable economic activity is, the smaller the benefits from a floating exchange rate in fostering adjustment are and the higher the costs in increased transaction costs and volatility are. Bernard Fortin's estimate that a separate Quebec currency could cost Quebec $40 billion if future costs are discounted to the present illustrates this point (Commission, 1991b, p.288).

The Bank of Canada has already gained the confidence of the international financial community for the stability of the Canadian dollar. Quebec would have to earn such confidence for its new currency. The only quick way to gain confidence would be to peg the Quebec dollar to either the Canadian or U.S. dollar. In so doing, Quebec would lose the capacity to conduct an independent monetary policy. Separation would definitely not be the road to monetary independence for Quebec.

Confrontation over the division of debt

On one issue, Quebec would have an advantage over Canada—the division of the $400 billion national debt. The debt is an obligation of the government of Canada. Quebec would have to be persuaded to assume its one-quarter proportional share based on population.

Currently, we are getting mixed signals from Quebec on how they propose to split the debt. Jacques Parizeau, the Parti Québécois leader, said in Toronto last December that "we will...haggle for a few weeks before we come to something like a quarter." But one of the background studies of the Bélanger-Campeau report argued that Quebec's share of debt should be only 18.5 percent based on federal assets and revenues in Quebec (17.5 percent if pension liabilities are included). The size of the deficit Quebec assumes will make the difference between an almost-balanced budget and a huge deficit. Each 1 percentage point share is worth roughly $4 billion.

There also seems to be some resistance in Quebec to the idea of replacing federal market issues with Quebec issues. The preferred option in Quebec is to leave the federal debt as it is and only to reimburse the federal government for the interest in order to avoid the unnecessary costs of issuing new bonds. But the unmatured debt outstanding has an average term to maturity of only four years. So it would be possible to refinance most of the debt in five to ten years without incurring additional financial costs. The real reason that it would be advantageous for Quebec not to have to assume directly its share of the debt is to avoid an increased risk premium for Quebec government securities. Also, it would strengthen Quebec's hand in future negotiations because Quebec would have the option of threatening to withhold payments if the bargaining were not going its way.

As a last resort, the federal government always has the extreme option of reneging on the roughly 17.5 percent of federal public debt held in Quebec. But this option would disrupt financial markets and it would undermine the federal government's credit rating. It would be used only if there was a complete and acrimonious breakdown of negotiations over the distribution of the debt.

A related issue would be the division of national assets. Presumably those federal government assets having a fixed location, such as buildings and land, would be assigned to Quebec or to the rest of Canada based on their location. But mobile assets would be subject to more disagreement. Breaking up commercially viable crown corporations would be controversial, and if not done carefully could lead to declines in output and employment. A fair split of assets and liabilities would require that all assets and liabilities be evaluated and that agreement be reached on a fair overall sharing ratio, such as population.

Reductions in the public service

The federal Public Service would have to be cut back sharply if Quebec were to separate, perhaps not by as much as one-quarter, which is proportional to Quebec's quarter population share, but certainly substantially. The impact would be greatest in the Ottawa area. Currently 53,000 federal public servants work on the Ontario side of the Ottawa River and 18,000 on the Quebec side. While some public servants in Quebec would be hired by the Quebec government, many public servants would become unemployed, including many of the 25,000 Outaouais residents with federal jobs in the Ottawa area. Unemployment would rise until displaced public servants could find new jobs. Property values in Ottawa could be expected to decline unless there was an inflow of people from Quebec. Hull and the Outaouais region would be even harder hit. Those remaining in Quebec could not expect to keep their federal jobs, and many would probably decide to move to Ontario. The closure of federal offices in Hull and the sale of homes by those moving to Ontario would produce a real collapse in property values.

Elimination of federal fiscal transfers

Quebeckers must recognize that they are a principal beneficiary of federal government fiscal transactions. Even the Bélanger-Campeau Commission estimated that in 1988 Quebec received a net fiscal gain of $409 per capita, or $2.7 billion, from its transactions with the federal government (Commission, 1991b, p.335). An independent Quebec would not get an equivalent amount of foreign aid from Ottawa.

The end of bilingualism

If Quebec were to leave Canada, it would probably mark the end of bilingualism in Canada. Canada has operated as a buffer between French-speaking Quebec and English-Speaking North America. An independent Quebec would have to deal directly with the United States without the accustomed support from Canada. French documentation and labelling would no longer be obligatory for suppliers of goods to Canada, eliminating a non-tariff barrier to trade. The Quebec economy would have to bear the full cost of language requirements itself.

Higher telephone rates for Quebec

Telephone rates are currently set by the CRTC for the whole Bell Canada region encompassing Ontario and Quebec. If rates were to be set separately for Ontario and Quebec, they would have to be increased substantially for Quebec because of the cross subsidy between toll and local service. Toll service costs only a fraction of the price charged to consumers; local service costs double the price. Since French-speaking Quebec accounts for only around 30 percent of the long distance calls in the Bell Canada region, telephone rates would have to increase sharply in a sovereign Quebec.

Territorial disputes

The most divisive issue of all is the territorial boundary of a sovereign Quebec. With the transfer of Hudson's Bay Company lands to Quebec under 1898 and 1912 federal legislation, Quebec's territory has grown since Confederation from 193,000 square miles to 595,000 square miles today. This territory includes James Bay and its hydroelectric facilities which have been central to the development strategy of a succession of Quebec governments. The federal government still has a strong legal claim on this territory under the terms of the transfer (Varty, 1991). Gordon Robertson has asked how the right of self-determination of the aboriginal people of this territory could be denied if Quebec were to exercise its own right of self-determination through a referendum (Robertson, 1991, p.B3). Other issues which could be raised are the possibility of a transportation corridor between the Atlantic provinces and the rest of Canada and the right of unimpeded access through the St. Lawrence Seaway. On the other hand, Quebec has made a claim to Labrador based on its rejection of the 1927 decision of the Judicial Committee of the Privy Council settling the Canada-Newfoundland boundary.

A territorial dispute would quickly turn negotiations over sovereignty sour; it would almost guarantee an acrimonious and mutually destructive split. Even the possibility of force and violence could not be ruled out. That virtually no countries have broken up without violence is worrisome.

Upheaval in the transition

The consensus among many Quebec economists and businesspeople as reflected in the Bélanger-Campeau report, is that in the long run, there would be no economic costs of sovereignty, and short-run transitional costs could be minimized if both sides to the split behaved rationally. This consensus is based more on wishful thinking than on facts.

The process of separation would be very costly. A strong central government in the rest of Canada and Quebec and sound economic policies would be necessary to control the damage. Even so, economic disruptions and hardship would be great. Many people would move from Quebec to Canada, adding to the flow of 200,000 anglophones who have left Montreal during the last 15 years. Property values in Quebec would be depressed. Confidence in the Canadian and Quebec economies would be shaken. Capital would flee the country until reined in by high interest rates. The stock market would dip and maybe even crash. The solvency of the financial system would be severely tested. Business investment plans would be shelved pending the resolution of the uncertainty. There could be at least a mild recession in Canada and a much worse one in Quebec.[2]

In addition to the dangers of balkanization, English Canada would have to guard against a nationalist backlash which could result in the introduction of interventionist and protectionist policies and an increase in fiscal deficits. These policies could transform the short-term economic costs of Quebec independence into long-run permanent losses. For its part and to its credit, Quebec seems to be committed to pursuing market-oriented and fiscally responsible policies regardless of the resolution of the current crisis (and in sharp contrast to Ontario). Quebec has been one of the biggest boosters of the Canada-United States Free Trade Agreement and is supportive of a trilateral pact with Mexico. Such sound and outward-looking economic policies strengthen its ability to weather the economic storms of separation.

Problems could arise for English Canada if the United States were to insist on renegotiating the free trade agreement with Canada if Quebec were to separate. The United States might try to tighten up the auto pact safeguards to the detriment of Canada's transplants or to gain improved access to markets for cultural industries. But the United States could also seek to extract these concessions within the context of the trilateral negotiations with Mexico. Quebec independence would not necessarily provide the U.S. with a unique opportunity to address outstanding grievances.

Disruption in the medium term and longer run

Once through the initial transition period, both Quebec and Canada would continue to be hurt.[3] It would take a long time to make up for the investment lost as a result of the crisis in confidence in the transitional period. Investment loss stemming from plant location decisions might never be regained. Furthermore, even a small risk premium in borrowing costs caused by Quebec's heavier debt burden and its currency risk could serve to dampen investment spending permanently and to reduce potential output.

There would also be the deadweight loss from the time and effort that the best brains and talents in the country would have to spend reorganizing and sorting out Canada's affairs. While this would strictly be a transitional cost, it would extend over such a long period that it could be considered a medium-term and even a long-run cost. More than 170 treaties govern Canada's relations with the United States. A similar web of treaties would have to be developed for Quebec and for Quebec's relations with Canada. Quebec would also have to negotiate many treaties with other countries to take the place of those that Canada already has. Negotiations can be very costly and time consuming. For example, the negotiation of the free trade agreement with the United States took more than two years, and during this period the Trade Negotiators Office had an annual budget of $10 million and employed more than one hundred people. The total cost of the negotiations, including expenditures for communications and for other departments, is estimated to be approximately $30 million by the time the trade agreement was implemented. Negotiations are not always as expensive as the free trade agreement. But to renegotiate 170 treaties with the United States and a similar amount with Quebec would be very costly. All the time and effort that would be required to negotiate and renegotiate treaties would be much better spent working to improve Canada's international competitiveness and other pressing domestic problems.

Quebec

In the long run, Quebec would probably continue to be much harder hit than the rest of Canada. Quebec is more dependent on trade with the rest of Canada than the rest of Canada is with Quebec (26.5 percent of Quebec's manufacturers' shipments went to the rest of Canada in 1984, compared to only 6.8 percent of the rest of Canada's shipments to Quebec). Quebec-Canada trade would be disrupted by the growth of barriers to the free flow of goods and services. Without a political union, it would be impossible to prevent a deterioration in the economic union.

Quebec's trade position is weak even as a part of, Canada. Its most important export industry—paper and allied products—is threatened by environmental concerns and regulations. Quebec's weak external position would be exacerbated by sovereignty. The importance of the vulnerable and highly protected "soft" sectors of textiles and clothing and furniture in Quebec manufacturing would accentuate Quebec's problem of adjustment. Quebec dairy farms, which provide almost half of the industrial milk for the country at a high price under supply management, would also definitely be at risk. Quebec would also lose access to a secure supply of petroleum. If a separate currency were established, increased transaction costs (estimated by Bernard Fortin to be 0.6 percent of GDP) would further cloud the trade picture. The only unambiguous strength of the Quebec economy is the export of hydroelectricity, but even it could be affected by territorial disputes with Canada and the James Bay Cree and by any efforts by Newfoundland to cut off Churchill Falls's power. Domestic sales of hydroelectricity to industrial users and the associated exports could also be curtailed if Quebec were forced to eliminate subsidies to reach a trade agreement with the United States.

Given the much higher degree of government intervention in the economy in Quebec than in the rest of Canada, Quebec might have difficulty negotiating a favourable free trade agreement with the United States. Quebec would also have less bargaining clout in international negotiations more generally. In any event, the external position of Quebec would be weak, and structural adjustment policies of the type advocated by the International Monetary Fund and World Bank would be required to strengthen the current account.

The Quebec economy has several weaknesses which would be exacerbated by independence. Quebec would lose the benefit of net fiscal transfers from the federal government. The budgetary deficit of the Quebec government would increase to well over $10 billion if Quebec were to take over the existing federal structure of revenues and expenditures. The loss of economies of scale in the provision of some government services such as defence and external relations could very well result in increased spending and an even higher deficit.

Net public debt as a proportion of GDP would rise from 35 percent of GDP in 1989 to 95 percent if Quebec's share of federal net debt based on population were factored in. Sharing federal public debt charges based on population, instead of on revenue as is currently the case, would increase public debt charges in Quebec by 0.7 percent of GDP, or $1 billion.

An independent Quebec would have a larger gross public debt than any of the seven largest industrialized countries except for Italy. Of the smaller countries, only Belgium and Ireland would have higher gross debt. A sovereign Quebec would definitely be a high public debt country.

International and domestic lenders could be expected to exact an interest premium from the Quebec government to compensate for the greater risk of lending to a high-debt sovereign Quebec, which they were doing until recently when support for sovereignty began to wane. The benefits that Quebec would be giving up, such as greater stability of revenues because of federal transfers, are recognized by lenders.

If Quebec were to lose the benefit of federal fiscal transfers and to assume its full one-quarter share of the federal debt, taxes would have to increase. An estimate of the required tax increase was offered in chapter 4 as 2 to 3 percent of GDP. This increase would be accentuated by the need for increased spending on health and pensions as the Quebec population ages. Fiscal belt-tightening would become the order of the day as structural adjustment policies were adopted to redress Quebec's weak external position.

If Quebec became a sovereign state, there would be a renewed exodus of the head offices of Canadian corporations out of Quebec. Quebec's business and entrepreneurial base would be further eroded. Canadian crown corporations such as Canadian National Railways, VIA and Air Canada would have no reason to be headquartered in a foreign country. Private firms such as Imasco, Montreal Trustco, and Power Corporation of Canada, which own Canadian financial institutions subject to restriction on foreign ownership, would under existing legislation be required to move their head office or divest. Similar restrictions apply to federally regulated telecommunication firms or their holding companies such as BCE Inc., Bell Canada, and Teleglobe, airlines such as Air Canada and broadcasting companies such Astral Inc. Other major firms such as Canadian Pacific, Seagrams Corporation, Molson and Alcan (and many smaller firms too numerous to name) might also decide to move. On the other hand, some Canadian firms may locate branch offices in Quebec as American firms have done in Canada.

Quebec's worsened growth prospects and its tax increases would encourage more anglophones to emigrate—almost half of whom have already expressed an intention to leave if Quebec were to become independent (Fontaine, 1991, p.A1). Emigration would further undermine Quebec's economic performance because of the key role anglophones play in the Quebec economy, particularly in maintaining links with the English-speaking North American business community.

However, while a sovereign Quebec would be worse off than it was as a Canadian province, it cannot be denied that Quebec would still have a viable economy. Quebec would not be the smallest country in the OECD if it were to become independent. Measured by GDP in U.S. dollars in 1988 converted at the average exchange rate, Quebec would only be slightly smaller than Austria and larger than Denmark, Finland, and Norway. In population Quebec would fit in between the same countries. Quebec's GDP per capita in terms of U.S. dollar purchasing power parity at $17,207 would make it the third highest income OECD country behind the United States and Canada. But, again, the real question for Quebeckers should not be whether a sovereign Quebec is viable economically, but whether Quebec would be better off economically.

A sovereign Quebec would definitely have serious adjustment problems, which could be addressed most effectively if business, labour, and government were induced by a crisis to work together for the greater good of a newly sovereign Quebec. The acceptance of a six-month wage freeze next year by Quebec public servants and the multi-year strike-free labour contracts at Aciers Inoxydable Atlas (Parent, 1991) and MIL Group Inc. (Gibbon, 1991, p.B3) provide examples of labour's willingness to cooperate in the current difficult climate. However, even a cooperative approach would not be sufficient to overcome the adjustment problems. Thus, a sovereign Quebec could still be in worse circumstances in the long run than Quebec the province, even if everyone cooperates in Quebec after separation.

The rest of Canada

The rest of the country would also be in worse circumstances in the long run if Quebec separates, but its situation would not be as bad as Quebec's. Key to the economic well-being of the rest of the country would be the need to resist centrifugal forces. Nevertheless, any reduction in access to the Quebec market would still have costs. Ontario and the Atlantic provinces would be most affected by any disruption in trade flows because of their greater dependence on trade with Quebec (8 to 9 percent of manufacturers' shipments from Ontario and the Atlantic provinces go to Quebec). The Prairies and British Columbia would be virtually unaffected (only 3.8 percent of manufacturers' shipments from the Prairies go to Quebec and only 1.7 percent from British Columbia). The so-called Pakistanization of Canada could particularly disrupt trade flows between the Atlantic provinces and the rest of Canada (8.9 percent of manufacturers' shipments from the Atlantic provinces goes to the rest of Canada and 1.8 percent from the rest of Canada to the Atlantic provinces). Given the higher proportion of trade which could be affected, the Atlantic provinces would be hurt the most by any disruption in trade.

Sharing the public debt will be critical in determining the long-run impact of Quebec's separation on the rest of Canada. For the impact to be relatively minor, Canada will have to ensure that Quebec assumes its full share of the debt.

A very serious disadvantage of Quebec separation for the rest of Canada would be the potential loss of international influence and prestige and the weakening of Canada's bargaining position in international negotiations. This loss could have an adverse effect on Canada's trade and on other economic relations with the United States and other major trading partners. But the significance of our weakened international position should not be overstated. Canada without Quebec would still be the seventh largest country in the OECD and would retain its status as a junior member of the G-7, though with reduced influence.

The cost of renegotiating treaties with the United States and of concluding similar treaties governing our relations with Quebec would be very high. The $30 million price tag on the free trade negotiations with the United States shows that treaties can be very expensive. Equally important, the negotiations would divert attention from other pressing issues that need attention.

Other institutional restructuring would also be required. Federal government policies and regulations are designed to be applicable to all of Canada. Canadian business operates in an integrated economy. If Quebec were to separate, the federal government would have to be restructured; many laws and regulations would have to be changed. Corresponding changes would be required in private sector firms. Financial institutions and other regulated industries like telecommunications would have to change the most. All of this change would be very costly.

On the positive side, Canada would benefit from the end of net fiscal benefits to Quebec from federal government transactions with the Quebec government and residents. Without Quebec, the recipient of almost half of equalization payments, the cost of fiscal transfer payments to less well-off provinces would be much more affordable for the deficit-strapped federal government.

The long-run economic impact of Quebec sovereignty on the rest of Canada would be conditioned as much by the policy responses of the Canadian government as by the direct impact of the act of separation itself. It would be important not to adopt protectionist and interventionist policies which would make the situation worse.

An estimate of the bottom line

Quantitative estimates of the economic impact of Quebec sovereignty on Quebec and the rest of Canada in both the short and long run are provided in table 37. It should be stressed that these estimates give only a rough indication of the orders of magnitude involved; they are not strictly additive. In addition, they do not take into account multiplier effects. Moreover, some important areas of impact are impossible to quantify and are thus only noted. It cannot be emphasized enough that the economic consequences of breaking up a county are so complicated and unpredictable that it is impossible to estimate them with any confidence. Nevertheless, in spite of their limitations, summary estimates are given to focus debate on the economic consequences of Quebec sovereignty.

The quantitative estimates highlight the fact that Quebec would be much harder hit than the rest of Canada if Quebec separates. Real output in Quebec could easily be depressed in the short run by as much as 10 percent and in the long run by 5 percent. In the short run, the output loss would be triggered by a crisis of confidence resulting from separation. In the long run, output loss would be caused by the required transfer of resources to the foreign sector (necessitated by the elimination of the existing fiscal gain in transactions with the federal government), by the emigration of anglophones, and by higher public debt charges resulting from the increased debt burden. The transfer would

TABLE 37

SUMMARY OF THE ECONOMIC IMPACT OF
QUEBEC SOVEREIGNTY
(Percent of GDP/(-) Loss and (+) Gain)

	Quebec		*Rest of Canada*	
	Short Run	*Long Run*	*Short Run*	*Long Run*
Trade				
- soft sectors	-1.2	small-	small+	small+
- current account	-2 to -3	-2 to -3		
- dairy	-0.5	small-	small+	small+
- Churchill Falls	-0.5	-0.5	+0.1	+0.1
Separate Que. currency	-1	-1	-0.3	-0.3
Existing Net Fiscal Gain	-2	-2	+0.6	+0.6
Public Debt Charges				
- Division of Debt	-0.7	-0.7	+0.2	+0.2
- Interest Rate Premium	-0.2	-0.2	0	0
Net migration	-1	-2	+0.3	+0.7
Confidence-induced Output Loss	-2.5 to -5	0	-2 to -3	0
Institutional Restructuring	large-	large-	large-	large-
Pressure for Protectionism and interventionist policies	small-	small-	large-	large-
Lost International Bargaining Clout	large-	large-	large-	large-
Elimination of Bilingual Labelling and Packaging	large-	large-	small+	small+

Note: Small is defined as being less than 0.5 percent of GDP and large greater than 1 percent of GDP. All of these items are not additive.

be made more difficult by the need to adjust in the soft and dairy sectors and by the probable loss of Churchill Falls's power, but it could be facilitated by increased taxes. The estimated impact of separation is very large: there is no policy that the Quebec government could pursue that could offset such a precipitous decline in output as that likely to be caused by separation.

For the rest of Canada, the economic costs which can be quantified are substantially lower than the costs for Quebec. And for Canada there are some offsetting economic gains. The net short-run costs would only be about one to two percent of GDP and would result mainly from the short-run loss of confidence caused by the separation of Quebec. The long-run quantifiable costs would be small—less than the quantifiable benefits. However, before English Canadians become too complacent about the consequences of Quebec sovereignty for the rest of Canada, it is important to stress that the estimates overlook three very important and costly items which defy quantification, namely institutional restructuring, pressure for protectionist and interventionist policies, and the loss of international bargaining clout. These costs would be sufficiently great to ensure a large economic loss for the rest of Canada from Quebec sovereignty.

A last warning

The economic costs of the separation of Quebec would be very high for Quebec. Although the costs are lower for the rest of Canada, they are still important, particularly the less tangible costs which are not readily quantifiable. Uncertainty over the eventual outcome of a split is one of the most important arguments against sovereignty. The Canadian economy is a powerful generator of wealth and jobs. It would be extremely foolish to break it up since Canada is not sure of the consequences.

Pointing out the costs of sovereignty is not to blackmail anyone. Rather it is to try to warn both Canadians and Quebeckers of the possibly dire economic consequences of their political choices in order to foster a needed spirit of compromise. If successful, it will spare much needless economic pain all around.

If the warning is not heeded, Canada will have to pull together to make the best of a bad situation. If Canada must establish economic relations with a sovereign Quebec, then Canadians must keep their emotions under control and be guided by self-interest, not spite. An emotional response would only make a bad situation worse. Damage control is the only rational response.

Notes

1. U.S. concerns in trade negotiations with a sovereign Quebec are discussed in more detail in Smith (1991) and Courchene (1991). The Quebec Inc. model is most fully developed in Courchene (1986).

2. Based on past recessions, the real output loss from the loss of confidence likely to be triggered by Quebec sovereignty could easily be in the range of 2.5 to 5 percent of GDP for Quebec and 2 to 3 percent of GDP for the rest of Canada. This range for the decline in output is based notionally on the 1981-82 and 1990-91 recessions. Another way of looking at it is that interest rates could rise by some 4 percentage points to stem capital outflows. The average impact of a 1 percentage point decrease in interest rates simulated with 9 macroeconomic models at a conference of model-builders was an increase in GDP of 0.2 percent in year 1 and 0.6 percent in year 3 (O'Reilly, 1983 and background papers). Assuming the impact of an increase in interest rates is the same magnitude and of opposite sign to a decrease and that model responses are linear, the impact of a 4 percentage point increase in interest rates would be a reduction of 0.8 percent in output in year 1 and 2.4 percent in year 3. To this impact could be added an additional reduction in investment resulting from uncertainty over sovereignty. Since business fixed investment in Quebec is around 11 percent of GDP, a 20-per-cent decline in business investment would amount to over 2 percent of GDP. A combination of the impact of interest rate increases and confidence-induced declines in investment could easily add up to an overall impact of 2.5 to 5 percent of output. This confidence-induced output loss would be exacerbated, especially in Quebec, by other output-depressing impacts.

3. John Helliwell and Alan Chung using a sophisticated econometric methodology have sought to quantify one aspect of the long-run impacts, the growth effects of national scale economies. They estimate that the growth in real GDP per capita would be reduced by 0.17 percent in Quebec and 0.06 percent in the rest of Canada (Helliwell and Chung, 1991, p.9). These are relatively small numbers and do not capture fully all the dynamic costs of breaking up the country.

References

Association des Economistes Québécois (1990) "Memoire au Bélanger-Campeau Commission."

Auer, L. and Mills, K. (1978) "Confederation and Some Regional Implications of Tariffs on Manufacturers," in Institute of Intergovernmental Relations and Economic Council of Canada, *Proceedings of The Workshop on the Political Economy of Confederation*, Queen's University, Kingston, Ontario, November 8-10, 1978.

Bank of Canada (1990) *Annual Report of the Governor* (Ottawa).

Beltrame, Julian (1991) "Bush expresses unity concerns," *The Ottawa Citizen*, March 14, 1991.

Boothe, Paul and Richard Harris (1991) "Alternative Divisions of Federal Assets and Liabilities," A Paper Presented at the John Deutsch Conference on Economic Dimensions of Constitutional Change, Queen's University, Kingston, June 4-6.

Brenner, Reuven (1991) "Canadian Choices," A Paper Presented at the John Deutsch Conference on Economic Dimensions of Constitutional Change, Queen's University, Kingston, June 4-6.

Caisse de dépôt et placement du Québec (1991) *Cycles et Tendance* Vol. IX, No.1 (Montreal).

Canada, Canadian Unity Information Office (1979) *The Textile Industry - A Canadian Challenge* (Ottawa: The Minister of Supply and Services Canada).

Canada, Canadian Unity Information Office (1978) *Trade Realities in Canada and the Issue of "Sovereignty Association,"* (Ottawa: Minister of Supply and Services).

Canada, Department of Finance (1977) "Statement by Mr. Macdonald on the Provincial Economic Accounts," June.

Canada, Department of Finance (1988) *The Canada-U.S. Free Trade Agreement: An Economic Assessment* (Ottawa).

Canada, Department of Finance (1991a) *The Budget* (Ottawa).

Canada, Department of Finance (1991b) *Quarterly Economic Review Special Report: Fiscal Indicators and Reference Tables* (Ottawa).

Canada, Department of Finance (1991) "Economic Linkages Among Provinces," *Quarterly Economic Review* March (Ottawa).

Canada, Office of the Prime Minister (1991a) "Notes for an Address by Prime Minister Brian Mulroney, Canadian and Empire Clubs of Toronto," February 12.

Canada, Office of the Prime Minister (1991b) "Notes for an Address by Prime Minister Brian Mulroney, Chamber of Commerce, Quebec City, Quebec," February 13.

Canadian International Trade Tribunal (1990) *An Inquiry into Textile Tariffs* (Ottawa: Supply and Services Canada).

Chambre de Commerce du Québec (1990) "L'Avenir Politique et Constitutionnel du Quebec: Sa Dimension Economique," le 7 novembre 1990.

Citizens' Forum on Canada's Future (1991a) *What We Have Heard So Far* (Ottawa).

Citizens' Forum on Canada's Future (1991b) *Report to the People and Government of Canada* (Ottawa).

Close, Patricia (1989) "Whither North America and Quebec: A Political Economic Study," October 20.

Commission on the Political and Constitutional Future of Quebec (1991a) *Report*.

Commission sur l'avenir politique et constitutionnel du Québec (1991b) Élements d'analyse économique pertinents á la révision du statut potitique et constitutionnel du Québec, Document de travail, numéro 1.

Conference Board of Canada (1991) *Provincial Outlook*, Vol.6, No.2.

Constitutional Committee of the Liberal Party of Quebec (1991) *A Quebec Free to Choose,* January 28.

Côté, Marcel (1990a) "Canada's Constitutional Future: A Viable Option," A Presentation to the C.D. Howe Institute Policy Analysis Committee, November 16.

Côté, Marcel (1990b) "Coping with Constitutional Uncertainty," November 20.

Courchene, Thomas J. (1986) "Market Nationalism," *Policy Options,* October, pp.7-12.

Courchene, Thomas J. (1991) "Canada 1992: Political Denouement or Economic Renaissance," A Paper Presented at the John Deutsch Conference on Economic Dimensions of Constitutional Change, Queen' University, Kingston, June 4-6.

Courville, Leon et al (1979) *La Sensitivité des industrie au commerce interregionale: Le cas du Québec, Ontario et du reste du Canada* (Québec: Editeur Officiel du Québec).

Delacourt, Susan (1991) "Give politicians the last word, committee says," *Globe and Mail,* June 21, 1991, p.A4.

Drohan, Madelaine (1991) "German Leader enters debate on future of Canada," *Globe and Mail,* June 17, 1991. p.A1.

Dudley, Leonard (1973) "Sur l'optimalité de la zone monetaire canadienne," *L'actualité économique* (janvier-mars).

First Boston Corporation, Economist Department (1991) "Constitutional Change," February 25.

Fontaine, Mario (1991) "L'indépendence ferait fuir 1 anglophone sur 2," *La Presse,* April 27, 1991, pp.A1-2.

Fortin, Bernard (1979) *Les avantages et les coûts des différents option monétaire d'une petite économie ouverte: un cadre analytique* (Quebec: Department of Intergovernmental Affairs, 1979, p10. (Translated by Maxwell and Pestiau, *Ibid,* p.37.)

Gibbon, Ann (1991) "Workers vow not to strike," *Globe and Mail,* July 5, 1991.

Globe and Mail (1991) "Hydro's controversial and costly policy," *Globe and Mail,* April 13, 1991.

Glynn, Anthony (1978) "The Net Provincial Expenditures Associated with Federal Government Expenditures and Fiscal Autonomy," in Institute of Intergovernmental Relations and Economic Council of Canada, *Proceedings of The Workshop on the Political Economy of Confederation*, Queen's University, Kingston, Ontario, November 8-10, 1978.

Gorham, Beth (1991) "Power Play: Bitter memories of a bad deal may poison the future of hydro in Labrador," *The Ottawa Citizen*, June 23, 1991, p.E6.

Hazledine, Tim (1978) "The Economic Costs and Benefits of the Canadian Federal Customs Union," in Institute of Intergovernmental Relations and Economic Council of Canada, *Proceedings of The Workshop on the Political Economy of Confederation*, Queen's University, Kingston, Ontario, November 8-10, 1978.

Helliwell, John and Chung, Alan (1991) "Are Bigger Countries Better Off?" A Paper Presented at the John Deutsch Conference on Economic Dimensions of Constitutional Change, Queen' University, Kingston, June 4-6.

Horry, Isabella D. and Walker, Michael A. (1991) *Government Spending Facts* (Vancouver: Fraser Institute).

Howitt, Peter (1991) "Constitutional Reform and the Bank of Canada," A Paper Presented at the John Deutsch Conference on Economic Dimensions of Constitutional Change, Queen's University, Kingston, June 4-6.

International Monetary Fund (1990) *World Economic Outlook* October 1990 (Washington, D.C.).

Ip, Irene K. (1991) *Big Spenders: A Survey of Provincial Government Finances in Canada* (Toronto: C.D. Howe Institute).

Julien, Germain et Proulx, Marcel (sous la direction de Arthur Tremblay) (1978) *Le chevauchement des programmes fédéraux et québecois* (Québec: École nationale d'administration publique).

Keynes, John Maynard (1920) *The Economic Consequences of the Peace* (New York: Harcourt, Brace and Howe).

Laidler, David E.W. (1990) "Money after Meech," C. Howe Institute *Commentary*, No.22 (September).

Macdonald, Don (1991) "Sovereignty will not end monetary ties, Parizeau vows," *The Ottawa Citizen*, May 28, 1991.

Mansell, Robert L. and Ronald C. Schlenker (1990) "An Analysis of Regional Distribution of Federal Fiscal Balances: Updated Data," unpublished paper, Department of Economics, University of Calgary.

Maxwell, Judith and Pestieau, Caroline (1980) *Economic Realities of Contemporary Confederation* (Montreal: C.D. Howe Research Institute).

McKenna, Barrie (1991) "Quebec credit upheld," *Globe and Mail*, June 27, 1991, p.B8.

Milner, Brian and Séguin, Rhéal (1990) "Warning issued on lending to Quebec," *The Globe and Mail*, March 14.

Montmarquette, C. and Dallaire C. (1980) "Le Rendement Des Obligations Provinciales et l'Incertitude Politique: une Analyse de Séries Chronologique," *L'Actualité économique* No. 3 (juillet-septembre), pp.388-404.

Mundell, Robert (1961) "A Theory of Optimum Currency Areas," *American Economic Review*, No. 51 (September).

O'Reilly, Brian, Paulin, G. and Smith Phil (1983) "Responses of Models to Selective Policy Shocks," Technical Report 38 (Ottawa: Bank of Canada).

Parent, Rollande (1991) "Reconciliation à la grève contre un investissement de 400 à Tracy," *Le Devoir*, 9 avril 1991, p.A-1-4.

Parizeau, Jacques (1990) "What Does Sovereignty Association Mean?" Notes for a speech to be delivered at a special joint meeting of The Empire Club of Canada and the Canadian Club, Toronto, December 11.

Parti Québécois, *La Souveraineté: Pourquoi? Comment?* (Montréal: 1990),p.3.

Picard, André (1991) "Quebec's economic heart needs stimulant," *Globe and Mail*, March 28, 1991.

Purvis, Douglas D. (1990) "The Bonds that tie," *Globe and Mail*, April 23.

Quebec, Ministry of Finance (1990) *1990-1991 Budget* (Quebec).

Quebec, Ministry of Finance (1991) *1991-1992 Budget* (Quebec).

Quebec, Ministry of Industry and Commerce (1977) "Presentation of the Economic Accounts of Quebec."

Raynauld, André (1990) "Les Enjeux Économique de la Souveraineté," Mémoire soumis au Conseil du Patronat du Québec, Octobre.

Reid, Angus (1991) "Polls Quicken the Pulse of Quebec," *Ottawa Citizen*, April 8, 1991, p.A1

Reuber, Grant (1990) "If Quebec seceded have-not provinces could really suffer," *Globe and Mail*, April 9, p.B2.

Robertson, Gordon (1991) "After 124 Years Canada is too Great a Country to Fail," *The Ottawa Citizen*, June 9, p.B3)

Smith, Murray (1991) "The Quebec Sovereignty Issue: Implications for Canadian Trade Policies," A Paper Presented at the John Deutsch Conference on Economic Dimensions of Constitutional Change, Queen' University, Kingston, June 4-6.

Task Force on Canadian Unity (1979) *A Future Together* (Ottawa: Minister of Supply and Services Canada).

Taylor, Joseph C. (1990) "Province of Québec Hydro Québec Moody's Aa3/S&P AA.," Merrill Lynch, February 23.

Toronto Dominion Bank, Department of Economic Research (1990) "Developments in Canada's Constitution: An Analysis of the Meech Lake Accord," January 1990.

Whalley, John and Trela, Irene (1986) *Regional Aspects of Confederation*, Royal Commission on the Economic Union and Development Prospects for Canada Study 68 (Toronto: University of Toronto Press).

Varty, David L. (1991) *Who Gets Ungava?* (Vancouver: Varty & Company Printers).

World Bank (1990) *World Debt Tables 1989-90*, (Washington).